BANK ON IT

BANK ON IT:

A Memoir of Tenure, Truth, and Tenacity

By
Darlene Winston

First Edition

LCCN 2025901690

ISBN   Hardcover 979-8-9910736-0-8
ISBN   Paperback 979-8-9910736-1-5
ISBN   eBook   979-8-9910736-2-2
ISBN   Kindle   979-8-9910736-4-6
ISBN   Large Print 979-8-9910736-3-9

bankonitmemoir@gmail.com

bankonitmemoir.com

Dedication

To Loraine, *my friend,* I dedicate this book to you

I often think about how much of me I lost when you died. It's as though half my soul died with you. I'm realistic; I know people die. As humans, we try to imagine life without someone; that's our nature. But in my wildest dreams, I never had a vision, a scintilla of a thought of you not being here. I just never imagined life without you—not that I selfishly took you for granted, but I surely took for granted that you'd always be here with me. I never thought about how vital you were to my everyday existence. I just always expected I would get up every morning, and you would just be there like my arms and my legs. Yes, I have my husband, children, grandchildren, and other family and friends, but I don't have you, *my friend.*

You were the keeper of my secrets, the person who knew me best. The person with whom I could be totally vulnerable and trust with my every thought. Over fifty years we stood together, raised our children together, supported each other's dreams, called out each other's bullshit, and supported each other without question. Whether we lived in different states or down the street, I knew you were there and that you had my back whether I was in the room or out of the room. Our friendship knew no bounds. I miss that, that unconditional acceptance and love.

Sometimes I hear or see something funny and I say, *Loraine would be cracking up at this,* and I can hear your laughter and see the expressions on your face. Or I have a conversation with myself, wishing I could talk to you, even though I know exactly what you would say because I can still hear your voice, your responses, your laugh, and your thoughts. The truth is that when you were here, we could and often did communicate across a room with just a look, never having to say a word. We knew each other's thoughts in almost every given situation. We simply knew each other that well.

At the end of the day, I just want to pick up the phone and hear your voice. Just to hear you say, "Hey gal."

I miss you so very, very much.

I pray that I gave you as much as you gave me.

Special Recognition to:

Anna Floit, editor, who was there from the beginning.

Dr. Jennifer Towne, developmental editor, who understood the assignment within ten minutes of our first meeting.

Ashley Hagan, editor, formatter, publishing consultant, my unexpected blessing who pulled it all together.

This would not have been possible without all of you.

Thank you.

Introduction

My expectations of reward for hard work don't come from a place of entitlement but from the interpretation of what society says we should do to succeed. Although I followed society's expectations, the same criteria for reward didn't apply to me as a Black woman in the banking industry. It was quite the opposite. I put in the work. I studied and got the credentials. I even got an Ivy League master's degree.

I stepped up to take leadership in the organizations I joined, leading every team in whatever the measurements deemed successful. I volunteered and gave back to the communities I was a part of. I have certifications and licenses in many fields. I looked good on paper, but none of it mattered in the grand scheme of things because I didn't have the connections.

Paradoxically, my leadership and successes also made people in power resent my strength (that hard enamel I learned to surround myself with). I never had a mentor, forerunner, or advocate in my forty-three-year banking career. When I tried to develop those relationships, I was shunned. Without a connection to the people in power, I had the difficult task of constantly raising my own banner and advocating for myself.

I now know that attending college is more about connections and less about education. As a Black woman, I've found those were the connections that would have gotten me a second look for an opportunity. The first is the look of disdain because I am Black. I was the perfect victim.

From the outside looking in, my family and friends saw me as a successful Black girl from the projects of Harlem who overcame a single-parent household and the bullying of my grandmother. I had my own car. I bought my first house at twenty-four. I custom-built two homes within ten years. I owned a total of four different homes throughout my life. I looked like the "American Dream," but nobody understood what I was enduring in the banking industry as a Black woman. They would never be able to imagine how I had to balance things in a way to get small wins for myself so that while I was being discriminated against and harassed, my small wins created my own version of the American Dream.

Instead of buying designer shoes and purses, I observed my White counterparts and traveled and bought houses. However, I never, ever forgot the social worker from welfare coming to our home and demanding we not have any "luxuries"—not a toaster, not an iron, not a man in the home—making sure we continued to be deprived and depressed of life's necessities. I was never going to allow that to happen to me, so I took the abuse and the bullying, believing I had no rights or recourse, never wanting to look back.

At all costs, I paid dearly.

Table of Contents

PART I: THE FIRST DEPOSIT

1
Banking on the Odds

My mother got pregnant with me at the age of seventeen, out of wedlock. Nana, my grandmother, was also pregnant. In 1958 it was an embarrassment to the family for a girl to be pregnant and unmarried, so double the embarrassment to the family. Nana had my aunt Caroline two months after I was born.

Both my grandmothers forced my parents to get married before I was born at ages seventeen and eighteen. But what seventeen-and-eighteen-year-olds do you know who have a clue about who they are, what they want to be in life, how to stay married, and how to parent? Exactly. It's no surprise that within three years of this union, my parents divorced.

Mommy was six months pregnant with my brother Andre when we moved back into Nana's house. As hard as I try, I can only remember flashes of things between the ages of three and ten. I remember lying next to Mommy on the couch and looking up at the big, round, black, and gold metal clock with candles on either side, and Mommy screaming. The police and ambulance attendants were all standing around us on the couch in Nana's living room, preparing to take her to the hospital. She was having the baby, my brother Andre. I had to be three years old because I am exactly three years and two days older than Andre. But, for the life of me, I don't remember Andre as a baby.

The next memory I have is when I was five years old. Mommy always walked me to school past the gas station down the street from the projects. Every day the man in the gas station came running out of the office, trying to talk to Mommy. "Hey Miss Lady, what's your name?" Mommy would just throw her head up in the air and didn't even answer him.

In all of Mommy's despair, she was proud and had a haughtiness about her, always telling me, "Darlene, nobody is better than you, and don't ever worry about what somebody has that you don't have." Perhaps that was her way of arming me, teaching me to build that hard shell around me to protect and defend myself from the barrage of bullshit she knew was coming my way, that I would have to use as fertilizer to survive. It is the one thing I will always remember about her: that stubborn pride. All three of us, her children, have it. *Oh, baby,* she could ignore a person like nobody's business.

"Mommy, that man is talking to you."

"Darlene, come on; I ain't studin' that man."

Finally, she started talking to that man, Albert, who later became my stepfather. By the time I was seven, Mommy and Albert had my little sister, Deborah—another person added to Nana's already overcrowded, two-bedroom apartment.

Automatic Telling Machine
Moving back into Nana's house, you would think that meant Caroline would have been my playmate and a sister for life. While we were raised as sisters and had our laughs, as children would, the dynamic of the home was certainly far from equal—or pleasant. We all lived with Nana in a two-bedroom apartment in the projects. This tiny box in the wall was crowded, most times with Nana, Mommy, me, Caroline, Andre, Deborah, my Uncle Melvin, and my Aunt Barbara.

This apartment was like an old homestead. I think my family thought there was some generational wealth in it if they held onto it. Nana moved into the apartment in 1942 when she left South Carolina. Mommy was two and Aunt Barbara was three. Although you could only legally have the people listed on the lease living in the apartment, Mommy, Aunt Barbara, and Uncle Melvin came back home to the two-bedroom apartment we all shared whenever their lives were not going right. Caroline never left until her daughter and son each took it over as they started having children. They finally gave it up sixty-seven years later in 2009.

Because we lived with Nana, technically it was her and Caroline's house. Mommy, Aunt Barbara, and Uncle Melvin were all well past grown. I always had to defer to Caroline's wishes and needs (after all, it was her house), and she embellished every situation to get her way—and we all knew Nana would take her side.

In many situations, we would hear Uncle Melvin saying, "Now Nana, you know Caroline is lying."

Nana would say, "So! You're a grown man arguing with a child. Melvin, you ought to be ashamed of yourself."

He would just say, "Yeah alright," and walk away. None of us would ever disrespect Nana or argue with her. The grown-ups just said, "Okay," and walked away.

As a child, on the other hand, I had to obey and do whatever the deed was without protest. Uncle Melvin and Mommy were very close because she raised him while Nana was out gambling. She washed and ironed his clothes, got him ready for school, and made sure he ate.

He would go to my mother upset, "Mabel, you know Caroline is lying."

She would say, "Melvin, don't get upset and don't worry about it. We know Caroline is a liar. Don't even let that bother you."

My stepfather, Albert, used to say, "Caroline could lie faster than a cat could lick his ass while he had his tongue right on it." But even he was placated and thought her antics were funny. The common theme in our house was that Caroline was a liar, and Nana would defend her or brush it off.

Many of the lessons I learned are ingrained in ways I didn't realize. I watched adults who had the power to change the situation walk away and not fight. They just walked away. They supped it. They lived with the lies they told themselves and the lies they were made to believe. *It really wasn't alright, but it was our reality.* They taught me not to go to the source but to make room for the problem.

The next time Mommy tried life on her own, we moved out of Nana's house to the Bronx on Washington Avenue. I can still remember the address: 1775 Washington Avenue. Mommy always made sure we knew where we lived. Mommy, Holly, and Carly (her cousins and best friends) were always there, drinking and dancing. For entertainment, they would put Andre on top of the radiator in the apartment and he would jump down and do the split like he was James Brown. Mommy was drinking bad by then.

We only lived there for a little while before we were back at Nana's house. I believe that it was during this time that Nana convinced the authorities that she was taking care of us and she should be the one getting the welfare check for us. Mommy hanging out and drinking had set Nana up good to get more money to gamble with.

2
My First Discriminator

Involuntary Bankruptcy

Nana did all her daytime gambling business lying across the twin bed in the second bedroom. Never in the main bedroom (Nana's room) with the big bed. That room always had to be cleaned and the bed made each morning. Most of my days started with Nana calling me.

"Darlene, come run roun' the corner and get me my newspaper. Hurry up now so you can get my numbers in before y'all leave for school." Caroline would be just dragging around the house. After bringing the newspaper back, I'd start getting ready for school. Nana called out again. "Darlene, y'all (as if she was speaking to me and Caroline, but I knew full well she meant me) come look for my glasses."

Looking under the bed and through the covers I'd turn and look at her. "Nana, you have them on your head."

She put on her glasses and also using her magnifying glass she'd start inspecting Ching Chow (a comic in the back of the New York Daily newspaper) in detail. I could hear Nana while I was getting dressed.

"Lord, Ching Chow is holding up a seven. Darlene, come here, that look like a seven to you?"

"Yes, Nana," I replied.

Nana would start writing her list of numbers on a piece of notebook paper folded in four columns. The list of three-digit numbers as long as the sheet of paper would fill the first column. Those were all for a penny. The next column would be filled about a quarter of the length of the sheet with the seven and some other single-digit numbers ranging from twenty-five cents to fifty cents. The seven was definitely fifty cents or more, and then she would have a list of double-digit numbers (called *bolitas*) for various amounts ranging from twenty-five cents to a dollar.

"Here, Darlene, run this up to Mike's; don't be late. When that seven comes out, Grandmama gon' git you something nice."

I was sure that seven would never come, and if it did, there certainly would be nothing "nice"—for me. *She knew she wasn't gon' buy me nuthin.' As soon as she hits she gon' buy something for Caroline like she always does.*

This was the way of life. Caroline was usually lying behind Nana in bed. They would be whispering about who knows what. I'd stand there, waiting for Nana to finish writing out her numbers as they acted like I wasn't there. I would be standing there screaming inside...*What about me? I wished that was me lying with them in that bed.* I wondered what they were talking about. I wanted so badly to be included in their secret. Thinking if I kept standing there, Nana would see me and call me over, but they just kept ignoring me. I'm not going to say anything and be disrespectful. Like Nana said, I'm a "good, big girl." *Maybe next time.*

Anyway, children are to be seen and not heard. It's okay. I'm not going to get upset and let them think they hurt my feelings. Plus, it's Caroline's house. It didn't matter that Caroline and I were the same age and *"big girl"* only meant taller. I was five feet and seven inches tall by the age of ten and only about eighty pounds soaking wet. I was always obedient. While I continued to push my feelings further down, Nana continued to remind me that I was a "big girl." It would always start with, "Now, Darlene, you be a big girl," especially in situations where she wanted me to understand why I must accept less than expected. And then it would be followed by the guilt statement, "You have to understand that your mother can't afford it; don't make her feel bad."

Life was life. Caroline got her way in every way, and I was left to be the "big girl" who was expected to shoulder the responsibility. While I had Mommy, Nana really ran the house, and everyone else was left to comply. This way of living ran me from the house. I loved everything outside of it— especially school. I was an "A" student, obviously smarter than the "D" student Caroline presented herself to be, and school was the one place where I controlled the best outcome for myself.

The Dancing Number: Prom, here I come

Like any teen in junior high school, I couldn't wait to go to prom and that's *alll* my friends and I talked about all year long. The time had come, and I knew my grades would permit me to go. I worked *so* hard.

When I saw that report card, baby, you would have thought I won my first Olympic gold medal. Running, shouting, waving my report card, Yes! Yes! Yes! A's down in every class. Oh yeah! Oh yeah! Oh yeah! I was dancing—rubber legging—my long skinny legs around to my own tune. I felt the rhythm through every fiber of my slender skin. I got A's. I'm number one; I'm number one; I am number one. Top of the class. Dean's List. I can't wait to go to the prom.

My victory celebration was interrupted by the ever-daunting "Darlene!" from Nana. I got out of my glory clouds to see what she wanted.

"Yes, Nana?"

Lying across the bed, Nana warned, "Come here. Now, you're smart. You're a big girl. You know your mother can't afford to buy you nuthin' for that prom." *Was she reading my mind?* I thought. I'm sure the look on my face said what I didn't dare say out loud.

The next thing Nana said took all the wind out of my sail. "Now, don't make your mother feel bad. Don't ask her if you can go to that prom." I walked away with my head hanging down. My skinny legs barely holding me up.

"Yes," I all but whispered. I didn't know *Crushed* had a name, but this was certainly it. My stomach hurt. My eyes watered. I could hardly breathe. My chest squeezed tightly inside me. I couldn't believe I was not going to the prom. My friends and I were all so excited. I knew they were going to ask me why I wasn't going. I just had to put on a brave face and say I changed my mind and didn't want to go.

I wondered what it would be like to go to a prom. What is it like to be important and wanted? I wonder how I would have looked all dressed up in my pretty, flowy, purple gown. I would have chosen purple to be different from everyone else. I'd have been waiting for the limousine to pick me up in front of the projects. My project friends were always supportive of me. I imagined them giving me high fives and hugging me as I made my victory walk down the tree-lined entrance of the projects to the limousine while all the grown-ups, happy to see a kid from the projects, who obviously graduated, looked out their windows to watch and cheer me on. They would have congratulated me and told me how pretty I looked.

My project friends were always happy and proud of me because even when they played hooky, I was the only one who still went to school. They didn't make me feel awkward or like an outcast. I guess I was their goody two-shoes. They always defended me, especially if somebody tried to tease me for going to school.

I would have been off to school for a night of fun. I would've gotten out of the limousine and met up with my school friends. We would have sashayed, modeling our gowns for each other, floating around the gym, and showing off our pretty purple, pink, blue, and yellow gowns. I know I would've stood out being the only one in purple. We'd have been whispering to each other about which boy we liked across the gym. I wanted *so badly* to be there.

They were going to have so much fun. Oh! How I wanted to be one of them. It must feel so good to be loved and be a part of the *in* crowd. I wished someone loved me that much. Nobody ever told me I looked pretty. This would have been the first time. I wished I was there.

This is not fair.

I silently knew in my heart that living with Nana and Caroline many things were unfair, but this was glaringly obvious. Nana had just told me the previous week that I couldn't go to my prom, but she bought Caroline *two* dresses for her prom, which was held the same day as mine. *Couldn't Nana have just bought me one? Why did Caroline need two?* Caroline was barely passing. Of course, one of those dresses was blue—Caroline's favorite color.

Once again my feelings were unchecked by anyone.

Hot Checks

Well, summer is here and life goes on. Aunt Barbara got married and moved off with her rich husband. Well, I don't know if he was rich, but he was rich by our standards. They occasionally came by to give Nana some money and bring gifts for Caroline.

Nana's gambling buddy, Ms. Ingrid, came by for her weekly visit to sell us clothes and play her numbers with Nana. We'd be outside playing at the sprinkler pond in the middle of the projects, and Caroline, out of nowhere, would take off running upstairs, faking a limp, and just as I would turn around to see what was happening, there would be Ms. Ingrid and her side-kick little Julio walking through the tree-lined entrance of the projects —the same entrance where I would have taken my victory walk to the limousine for my prom, *had I gone*—lugging two big red and white shopping bags and two shopping carts. *Shoot!* I was stuck again. Caroline always disappeared as soon as she saw Ms. Ingrid.

As they walked toward us at the sprinkler pond, Ms. Ingrid had already started her moaning, "Oye, Oye, Oye, Lordy help me." She had one big, red and white bag in her hand and another on top of one of the overflowing shopping carts. "Oye, Oye, Oye, Lordy help me," she repeated. Little Julio was weighed down with the heaviest and bulkiest of the bags and the other shopping cart. I felt so sorry for little Julio.

Ms. Ingrid was at least six feet tall and about three hundred pounds, dressed in her usual colorful outfit of reds and oranges with a turban on her head. Little Julio was all of five feet tall with pants too big and a rope for a belt tied tightly to hold them up. He always had a bottle of wine in his back pocket, head hanging low, looking down and sad, while he waited for Ms. Ingrid to bark out another order at him. I never heard him speak. I don't think he spoke English.

Good thing my friends knew me, otherwise I would have been the joke of the projects. Ms. Ingrid flopped down on the bench right in front of the sprinkler pond and started pulling sandwiches and other food from her bags.

Was she serious?

Everybody in the projects knew Ms. Ingrid was going to our house. Despite it being a New York City housing project, we were a small community, and we all knew each other. I was embarrassed for myself, even if my friends weren't. "Here!" she barked, handing little Julio a smaller portion of the food while she kept the bigger portion.

Nana yelled out the window, "Darlene y'all help Ingrid bring them bags upstairs!" Oh my God! Let's just make a public service announcement. I was already embarrassed; that quickly changed to mortified. Caroline was already upstairs with Nana, pretending her fake limp, so why did Nana say *y'all* when she really meant me? I was the only person left outside. I'm sure with Caroline lying in bed behind her, Nana was up there laughing and saying, *Poor Caroline* like she always did when she knew Caroline was lying. It was the same thing every week. Caroline would fake like she was sick, while I made two or three trips up and down the stairs to our third-floor apartment—two flights of seven stairs each to each floor—hauling Ms. Ingrid's junk. *I can't wait 'til I'm grown. I can't fit any of that stuff anyway. They make me sick.*

Ms. Ingrid always had new clothes stuffed down in the bottom of her bags with other things on top of them. Back then, we went shopping on Park Avenue, as we called it. It was under the El (the city's elevated train), the length of six city blocks and about a quarter of a city block wide. It was like walking through a tunnel. The vendors were on either side while shoppers maneuvered single file down the center. It was always crowded. I imagined Ms. Ingrid barreling through the crowd yelling out, "Oye, Oye Oye; Lordy, help me," with little Julio trailing behind her and shoppers mashing themselves together in the already cramped space trying to get out of her way, while the vendors frustratingly waited for her to move along and stop interrupting their sales. In retrospect, it could have been a perfect situation for pilfering.

Nana lay across one twin-sized bed, and Ms. Ingrid sat on the other twin bed. Ms. Ingrid always made little Julio sit in the living room. Although unspoken, no men—except Uncle Melvin and Andre—were ever allowed in the bedrooms. Ms. Ingrid pulled clothes from her bags one outfit at a time while Caroline and I went back and forth between Nana's big bedroom and the other bedroom trying them on. Each time we came into the bedroom to show them if the clothes fit, Ms. Ingrid would pull something else out of a bag. "Here! Try this on," as she threw another outfit our way. Because of my height, I rarely got any of the good stuff. Caroline, at five feet and two inches, got that stuff. I would get an occasional pair of shorts or a longer dress that was always ill-fitting because they were made for someone of average height. When Caroline and I finished trying on all the clothes, Nana and Ms. Ingrid would start haggling. Money was always tight, and Nana always had to pay Ms. Ingrid "next week" for any of the clothes we got from her.

They would start with Nana saying, "Ingrid, what I owe you?"

Ms Ingrid would reply, "Give me ten dollars for that dress and I'll throw in those pants for another five."

Nana would answer, "I'll give you twelve for both. Come by next week when I have my card game and get it."

"Okay, you cow." (Ms. Ingrid's pet name for Nana.)

Ms. Ingrid would then go into the living room and lay on the sofa. Little Julio would lie on the loveseat, and they would take a nap waiting for the first number to come out. Once everything settled down from Ms. Ingrid's visits, I always had the same impending thought that I gotta get out of here. I can't wait until I am grown. I am going to buy all of my clothes from a store.

The Guarantor

Living with Nana was precarious, and I learned some real-life lessons on what I would never do. There was a roof over our heads, but what a roof it was. In the 1960s and early 70s, if you were Black and on welfare, the social worker would come to your house and inspect it to make sure you didn't have a man living in the house and you didn't have any items they deemed a luxury. If you did, then it was decided you didn't need to be on welfare, and you would be kicked off. In hindsight, I can now see these were some of the ways the Black family structure was destroyed. Why was it deemed a luxury to have a Black father in the home?

The social worker would be coming up the stairs as we were frantically stuffing clothes and extra pots and pans in closets and under beds, clearing out any sign that we were enjoying any of the "luxuries" of life. Nana would be lying across the bed from her perch yelling in her Southern dialect, "Y'all put that toaster and iron and ironing boarding to the back of that hall closet! Git Melvin's clothes and put 'em' under dem' (them) beds somewhere!"

As the social worker knocked, Nana would get up, rushing to answer the door. Her last command before letting the social worker in was, "Y'all don't answer any questions and don't say a word." Caroline and I standing side-by-side, looking stone-faced. Mommy standing with Nana as the social worker walked around the house to perform an inspection. Doors to closets were opened. Kitchen cabinets were opened and slammed shut. In a loud and intimidating voice, dark and direct questions were spewed.

> "Do either of you have a man who visits?"
> "No, Uh-uh."
> "What time do the children go to school?"
> "8:00."
> "Who gets them ready?"
> "We do."
> "What did you eat for dinner last night?"
> "Chicken, vegetables, and rice."
> "Did you eat anything from a restaurant?"
> "No."
> "Okay, we'll see you next month."

The door slammed behind her. We let out our breath in unison and realized we were not breathing at all. The release of tension followed the social worker down the stairs. Whew! Nana would go back to laying across the bed and start yelling, "Y'all git that stuff outta dem (out of them) closets and put 'em back."

I knew then I wasn't ever going to be on welfare, having somebody come into my house asking questions and telling me what I can and cannot do, say, or have. Never gonna happen.

Gambler's Ruin

"Darlene, go next door and give this note to Ms. Jones."

Me returning, handing Nana a note from Ms. Jones. "Nana, Ms. Jones said to give this to you."

"Ok, now run this note up to Mike's for me. Come and dial Judy's (her sister) number before you go."

"Yes, Nana "

"Nana, Mike said to tell you he can't do it today."

I think Nana done gambled away the rent money. Nana was lying across the bed sniffling, yelling at us. "Y'all run roun' the corner and get some boxes and get this house packed up." No explanation, and we didn't dare ask. Children did what they were told.

I don't think she could borrow the money from anybody. Looking out the kitchen window, staring at the sprinkler pond, and daydreaming, I wondered where we'd go. I spotted bossy Aunt Judy coming up the walkway.

We knew Aunt Judy had to have money; she was the only person we knew who had a gold front tooth. Now we gon' have to clean up the whole house, from top to bottom, and promise to be at her church on Sunday. *I hoped we don't have to move the furniture around.*

"Y'all open that doe' (door) for Judy."

I opened the door. "Hi, Aunt Judy."

Also in her Southern dialect, "Gal, it's 10 o'clock; you ain't comb yo' (your) hair yet." *She startin' her mantra already.*

"Sweet (her nickname for Nana), you gotta stop all this gambling. Sweet, you don't make these kids do nothin'. This house ain't never clean. Sweet, you know you ought to be ashamed of yo'self. You don't even make these kids go to church."

Nana said, "You right, Judy; I'm gon' do better."

"Sweet, I can't keep giving you money."

"I know."

"Y'all bring that broom in here and sweep under this year' (here) bed."

"Yes, ma'am".

"I shouldn't have to come all the way up here to tell y'all to clean this house. Y'all gals too big for this."

Caroline jumped in the bed behind Nana, complaining that she didn't feel good. Aunt Judy laughed, "Caroline get yo' tail up and get them dishes cleaned up."

They all thought Caroline's lying and antics were funny. I imagined rolling my eyes so hard at them that my eyes got stuck in the back of my head. We ain't never going outside now.

"I gotta go. Y'all be in church at nine o'clock Sunday morning."

"Ok, Aunt Judy."

"And Gal, make sho' that head of yo's is combed."

"Yes ma'am."

"Y'all unpack that stuff and get this house cleaned up."

"Yes, Aunt Judy."

I closed the door behind her as Nana yelled from the bed, "Darlene, come and run my numbers up to Mike's!"

It looks like we're staying. And Nana ain't stopping her gambling

3
The Negative Balance

I always loved Mommy, but there were times when my anger toward her got the best of me. Because of her relationship, or lack thereof, with Nana, I sometimes got a shadow of her existence. I wanted Mommy to be there for me and to speak up when Nana treated me less than. I wished she'd comfort me, but that required seeing that I was hurting. Although she didn't have it any easier with Nana, I was still so angry that she didn't ever stand up for me.

I watched Mommy shrink away. She was like a wilting flower drowning from too much water, and Nana was the gardener who just kept pouring on more and more water. The water was the guilt Nana poured onto Mommy daily for getting pregnant at seventeen, out of wedlock, and embarrassing the family. Mommy just kept trying to bloom, doing anything Nana wanted, trying to be recognized and forgiven by her mother.

Nana was out gambling most days and nights. It seemed like Mommy's penance was to be responsible for all the chores around the house and raising me, Andre, Deborah, Caroline, and Uncle Melvin. Mommy was doing everything she could to be in Nana's good graces. She appeared to resolve herself to being the caregiver and homemaker. It was all she did for the rest of her life. She rarely laughed or smiled. Her dreams of becoming a hairstylist and owning her own shop had long gone down the drain with every load of clothes she washed.

I would imagine just hugging her so tight and saying, "Mommy everything is going to be okay. I'll take care of you."

At thirteen, I got my first job and begged Mommy to take my first paycheck, *it was only $37.50, but she deserved it,* and buy herself something nice. A slip or anything. She refused. This was my first acknowledgment and acceptance of the responsibility to take care of and protect my mother. Later in life when I was able to do more, she still rejected my every offer.

On the first and fifteenth of each month, the welfare checks came (Mother's Day as it was affectionately called in the hood).

We always took taxis—Mommy didn't ride buses. Mommy would take me shopping with her to Park Avenue to buy the groceries. She always let me pick out something (clothes) nice for myself, too, and I always got my favorite vanilla or strawberry sandwich wafer cookies, and she always bought a bottle of Barton's Reserve. We would then go visit Uncle Henry and Sissy (Nana's brother and sister-in-law). They would start with the bottle of Barton's Reserve Mommy bought, and by the end of the day, someone would have gone out to the store and bought at least two more bottles. Mommy was always so happy there. There was lots of laughing, drinking, and dancing. Sissy was like her mother, always giving mommy advice and making her feel good about herself. We always wound up spending the night there. Soon Mommy started going out more often, visiting and drinking with other friends. Most times she took me with her. I didn't mind; I wanted to make sure she was alright. She was always so sad at Nana's house. For a two-year period Mommy was in and out of the hospital. It was like she was having a nervous breakdown. I would sit with her through several hospital stays. By the time I was eighteen, Mommy had a bout of delirium tremens and stopped drinking for good.

4
My Asset Protection Plan

I can say I was certainly living a double life. While living through the pain and turmoil at Nana's house, I got a kind of reprieve on many weekends when visiting my father. Whereas I had my bout of anger with Mommy, Andre was always angry with Daddy. The constant chatter in Nana's house about how Daddy left Mommy six months pregnant with him was always the source of his anger. He could not accept that Mommy and Daddy were never in love but had to get married due to their circumstances.

Andre was also one of Nana's favorites. He always ate up all of the negativity that Nana constantly dished out. He ate up everything she said and was duly rewarded with laughter and love from Nana. She liked referring to him as "that's my boy." Perhaps by my demeanor, although obedient, I didn't buy any of the crap Nana laid down. I just *yessed* her to death and planned my great escape out of there.

While Andre lived with the pain of perceived rejection from the womb, I was the biggest daddy's girl. I had no ill will in my heart toward my father. I also clearly understood how controlling Nana could be, so I didn't fault Mommy for obeying. It was a condition of living with Nana. It was her way and her way only. I've always had an uncanny knack for seeing through the smokescreen people tried to hide behind when camouflaging the motives for their actions. *It's the one thing people dislike about me. The ability to see through their bullshit and my directness for calling them out on it.*

I didn't care how much Nana tried to turn us against Daddy; that sour plan was not working with me. Not only was she *not* going to keep me from loving my father, but she also was not going to keep me from seeing him, either.

On the rare occasions when Mommy and I would talk about Daddy, she'd say, "Darlene your father always loved you. He loved you more than he loved anybody else. When you were little, he would come home from work every day and just pick you up and hug you. He was always hugging you and kissing you and no matter what, on every Friday, payday, he always bought you something."

Later in life, I remember dating a guy who saw me hugging my father. He asked, "Do you and your father hug every time you see him?"

I said, "Every chance I get." (Looking back, I recognize my father's arms were my place of protection).

Though my mother and father divorced after three years, Daddy always owned up to his responsibility. Even at the age of eighteen, my father was not a deadbeat dad. He worked two jobs to take care of his wife and baby.

Three years after my parents divorced, my father remarried. He continued to be active in Andre's and my life while creating a new life with Lilly, his new wife, and eventually my brother Grant, their son together.

I spent as many weekends as possible with my father, and boy, did I get backlash from Nana for that. Being raised in a home by all women—Nana, Mommy, and sometimes Aunt Barbara—there was no male influence. Uncle Melvin had already gone off to college. Whenever I asked Mommy for something, Nana would step in and overshadow Mommy with one of two responses, "Your mother can't afford it," or she would say to my mother, "Mabel, let her go and ask her father since she loves him so much."

When I was with Daddy, Lilly would step in when she could and stop him from doing things for me. Whenever I went back home after a visit with Daddy, Mommy would curse my father, angrily, screaming at him, "Don't be letting your damn wife touch my daughter's hair!"

Even in my seven-year-old mind, I questioned, *how else was my hair to get done if I was there for the weekend?* I had very coarse long hair, and as soon as Daddy and I walked through the door, Lilly and her friend Tessa acted like I was a doll and they were playing house. They would sit me on a high stool in the kitchen of their tiny apartment. Lilly waited with the hot straightening comb in her hand as Tessa unbraided the braids Mommy had just put in my hair. They would always play in my hair and try out different styles. Tessa would say, in her sing-song voice, "Lil, you reckon when you have a little girl she will have hair like this?" I didn't see anything wrong with it then, but perhaps Mommy had a point about my hair, though it felt more like Nana was egging Mommy on about Daddy having a new wife. I guess fighting with Daddy about my hair was an easy fight for Mommy to pick if it made Nana happy.

Early on I learned not to fight my battles. I remember at thirteen making a conscious decision. I was not going to let them (Nana, Mommy, or Lilly) come between me and Daddy. I was not going to tell them anything we did when I came back from his house; I was not going to ask Daddy for anything so Lilly wouldn't get mad at him; and I didn't ask Mommy for anything so she wouldn't feel bad. That way everyone could be happy, Daddy would be safe from the vipers, and we'd be free to love each other without judgment.

I also decided I would not let anybody see how much I was hurting. I decided to just keep going about my business and acting like I was okay. I could work and get my own things. They wouldn't even know I was sad inside. "I'm smart, I'm a big girl." No one ever knew then or knows now the turmoil I sometimes feel inside. *It is a true balancing act to keep everyone happy while maintaining the façade that I am okay.*

Daddy would always catch me off guard, though, and say, "You okay, Babe?" Like he knew I wasn't. He seemed to always pick up on when I wasn't okay. I would sheepishly smile and force out the lie I believed would keep me protected. I would simply utter *yes* through my teeth. I had to often remind myself, *Don't forget to smile around Daddy.* I did not need my vulnerability found out.

When Daddy would come and get me for the weekend. We would always stop off somewhere before we got to his house and he would buy me something. He never said it, but I knew that it was our secret. When it was something big he would just say don't say anything, but I already knew I wouldn't. I never did. I was never going to get him in trouble. He didn't have to tell me not to say anything. I'd already decided in my heart that no one, including me, would ever jeopardize our relationship, the love I felt for him, and his willingness to express his love for me. Sharing secrets with Daddy was my secret joy.

My height provided me with big feet to match. Daddy was also tall, and he knew where all the stores were for tall sizes. He would come to get me to buy my shoes to start the school year. I would hop in his car excited, happy to be with Daddy, but also happy to be getting something that actually fit my long, slender build.

On one particular occasion, when Daddy came to get me, as I got into the car, he said, "We are going to the house to pick up Lil (his pet name for my stepmother), and then we'll go and get your shoes." When we got to his house he yelled upstairs.

"Hey Lil, you ready?"

She yelled back down, "We're not doing that today. I have other plans."

Daddy looked so confused by her response. I wasn't confused or surprised; *we should have just gone by ourselves.* I was so used to getting my hopes up and being let down that I already knew I had to sacrifice my wants for the peace of the moment.

I swallowed my disappointment like usual and said, "It's okay, Daddy. I can use the ones I have for now."

I had to remind myself to fix my demeanor to make it appear that I wasn't as hurt as I felt. Daddy apparently had mixed emotions, too. His face went through a myriad of expressions from irritated to embarrassed to frustrated. I was sure they had discussed this before I had gotten there, and he had no idea what these "plans" were, or more, where they came from out of nowhere. Daddy was a peacekeeper like me, but he still made sure I felt special. "Babe, we'll get your shoes later." I knew he would make good on his word. He always did. I also knew it would become another one of our secrets. This time, I could truly smile, because his words to me were worth their weight in gold.

Smiling, I replied, "Okay, Daddy."

Daddy seemed to be performing a balancing act of his own. He didn't want to go against his wife, piss off his ex-wife, disappoint his daughter, or further ostracize his son. He did everything possible to keep all of his relationships intact. I don't know if either of us succeeded, but I can say I always appreciated his commitment to his relationship with me despite the tightrope he had to walk while doing it. I didn't care what Nana, Mommy, or Lil did or how it fared with them. That was not my concern. I was committed to not letting any one of them stop me from being with my father. I didn't care how much they tried to hurt me with their antics, I was going to use it to my advantage. I was sure I could keep everyone happy. "I'm smart. I am a big girl."

Availability Policy

Nana was good at making sure I toed the line and making sure I felt guilty for being or even wanting to be happy. One day when my boyfriend Darryl walked me home, we stood in front of the apartment door, kissing. Nana opened the door, turned her head looking back into the apartment, and yelled, "Mabel, y'all better watch this gal!" As she looked back at me, she shook her head in disgust.

"Oh. My. God. This gal gon' get pregnant. She out here French kissing this boy." *What?*—I questioned myself often about the things Nana said. Did she really think I didn't know that this is not how you get pregnant?

It only got worse. On the days Nana let Darryl come into the house, we'd be sitting on the couch being innocent teenagers. After walking around checking on us to make sure the doors were open and definitely no French kissing was happening. At 10 p.m., Nana yelled out, from her bedroom, "I don't want no men in my house after ten o'clock!"

Oh my God! I couldn't believe she'd just done that. What in the absolute fuck! She was constantly embarrassing me in front of him. Darryl didn't say anything but just got up and left. He was always so nice and never made me feel bad about anything.

The next day at nine, she yelled from her bedroom, "I don't want no men in my house after nine." Jesus, really, lady. I can't do anything in this house. There was no pleasing her. *She always tryna' (trying to) make me look bad.*

The next day at eight, Nana yelled from her bedroom, "I don't want no men in my house after eight." It could be noon and she would say the same thing. The next day at seven, Nana yelled out, "I don't want no men in my house after seven." It was a dreadful week. I knew then I wasn't inviting him inside the house anymore. After that fiasco, I started going to Darryl's house after school.

Daddy was very active in our lives and was always advocating on our behalf for something or another. He would go anywhere and confront any situation on behalf of his children, whether it was driving from New York to North Carolina to get Andre into college and on the basketball team of his dreams, or checking in on our well-being.

One day I took my usual after-school route to Darryl's house. As I walked in, Daddy was sitting there, in Darryl's living room, talking to, or rather interrogating his father.

My fourteen-year-old insides were boiling hotter than a Louisiana fish fry. *Shit! Shit! Shit!* A million thoughts rushed through my head all at once. My slender frame never had any blood pressure issues, but I would bet every vein in my body was visible due to the amount and rate of blood pushing through them. *What was Daddy doing here? How does he even know where Darryl lives? What the fuck?* That damn Vivian Mason (Nana). It could only be her trying to sabotage the one ounce of happiness I experienced. As if her constant embarrassing me was not enough, she had to take her quest to shame me even further.

As though I had not walked in, Daddy's interrogation continued without interruption. "How do you monitor and observe your son and my daughter when they are in your home?" *Wait, what?* I never heard Darryl's father's response because by then I was struck numb, mortified, paralyzed, stuck in my tracks. The next thing I heard Daddy say was, "How do you protect my underage daughter when she's in your house?"

I must have blacked out in my mind's eye. I don't remember anything after that except leaving with Daddy. I loved Daddy tremendously, but my stomach had become the feet I had to walk on. I was petrified with humiliation. While I was grateful he cared, I was not used to *this* much care. I thought I had finally found my way around Nana embarrassing me with her antics in front of Darryl, and then this. This coupled with Nana's embarrassing, "I don't want no man in my house" routine. I knew if Darryl accepted me after this fiasco, he was the one for me, but I was sure he would definitely not be my boyfriend anymore. What in the world was he going to say to our friends? I couldn't help feeling the weight of my embarrassment.

As I walked out with Daddy, I faced an entirely new set of uncertainty. How did he know I was coming here? How long has he been here? What else does he know about me? I had never made Daddy angry before or to have him question my judgment. I mustered up the courage to start my questions at the beginning. "How did you know where he lived?" I asked Daddy.

"I know everything about you. I have people watching ya'll all the time. You don't do anything I don't know about. It's my job to protect you, *Darlene!*" Daddy replied with firmness. Great. Now I'm being spied on. God, I'm never going to be able to do *anything*.

I must be in another world. Darryl must think I am a fucking moron. I can't believe Daddy came here. How did he even know I had a boyfriend? How did he find out where he lived?—*that was rhetorical*. I knew Nana called him and told him. *I can't never have nothin'*. Nana made it her mission to torture me, and I was mortified. Oh. My. God. I was never going to live this down.

I now appreciate Daddy going to Darryl's house and showing up as the protector he had always been for me. The truth of the matter is, that I liked Darryl (a lot), but I mainly went to his house to dream. He lived in the new high-rise development in Harlem with balconies that overlooked the Hudson River. I would dream that one day I would live in an apartment like that with a view of the river. While I loved the view and dreamed of what life would be like living at that level, my ability to dream came to a screeching halt. Darryl died shortly after this. His parents never disclosed what happened to him.

I didn't know it then but the stars certainly had other plans for me.

5
Change in Interest

The year just flew by. It was the start of another summer. Gone were the days of playing in the sprinklers in the projects. Also gone were the days of daydreaming at Darryl's house of a different life.

During the hot Harlem summer afternoons, I hung out with my friends on the park bench many blocks from the projects. Away from Ms. Ingrid's visits and Nana's embarrassing antics and prying eyes.

The sun was high at ninety-six degrees, there was no breeze, and the heat felt like it was rising from the asphalt. That's when the most delightful-looking piece of human I'd ever seen turned up the temperature outside. Gordon walked into the park, and I think I started salivating. He was tall and muscular, had on a sleeveless t-shirt, and sun glistened off his biceps. He looked like he was fresh from the gym the way the sweat dripped off his muscles. Once I got to know Gordon I realized the sweat was just from the heat because Gordon was not ever going to exert himself in a gym. I found out he was eight years older than me. Never one to not go after what I want, needless to say, I made sure to get his attention, and that started our history together.

Our daughter Brandi was born when I was sixteen. I graduated high school at seventeen with a full scholarship to the Fashion Institute of Technology (FIT). I attended school full-time and worked part-time, and a few years later, Gordon and I got a one-bedroom apartment and moved in together.

6
Reflections of Wisdom

Cashing Checks

There were key messages given to me that shaped my reality of who I was.

The words by Daddy, Nana, and Mommy shaped the trajectory of my career, my personal life, and my frame of the world. Daddy would say, "Darlene, step up to the plate because always, and in every situation, someone has to lead, and that someone may as well be you." Those words imprinted on my soul, to me, translated to mean *take the lead* and *be responsible*. Nana had a way of drilling this "big girl" ideology into me every chance she got. The ideology certainly benefited her more than it ever did me, but that was a gamble she was willing to take. Her consistent message for me was that I was a "big girl." Those words made me believe I should shoulder all the responsibility, figuratively and literally, because I was a "big girl" every time and in every situation. Mommy's message, in her apparent despair, whether consciously or subconsciously, was that she couldn't or wouldn't defend me. Mommy's well-meaning words of wisdom, the one tool she offered me, "to never think that anyone was better than me," got snuffed out because I was treated like everyone was better than me. Her message, although it appeared to be no message of guidance, no impartation of wisdom, no nurture or truth, it actually taught me stoicism. Her message, though subliminal or silent, taught me to be stoic, understanding that dwelling on uncontrollable external events is futile. Instead, focus on my inner strength and resilience. Her silence spoke loudly and made her absence visible. I didn't need an interpreter to comprehend that I was on my own and not worth the risk of her being further bullied by Nana.

The lines in all three messages were certainly blurred as a child and young adult, but they each led me back to the same course of action. In every situation, I was expected to take on all responsibility, and because of my physical size, my feelings and needs didn't count. Because my inner needs were disregarded, I wasn't allowed to have boundaries or rewards. I was the one who was expected to help everyone else uphold theirs. I was responsible for and expected to make sure everyone was happy and cared for. These core messages put me on a mission to be a machine. No matter what anyone deposited, I had to make sure their check was cashed. With interest. With each transaction, I felt more and more robbed.

I carried these words with me into adulthood. They were pillars of my personal and professional life. These three messages fueled me and took the wheel to drive my career and life. The messages forced me to become an overachiever determined to overcome any obstacle while also being a victim who was taken advantage of, and I did not trust anyone to care for me or my well-being.

In trying to be a "big girl" and appease everyone, I was taught to be dependable, respect authority, and do the "right thing" by following all the rules. These behaviors should have yielded me rewards, or at the very least a path to the "American Dream," according to societal standards, but they didn't. Instead, I was victimized and taught not to defend myself. I was missing the necessary connections. The "be a big girl" lesson failed me at every turn, beginning at home with my grandmother, my mother, and my father.

The mindset of these thoughts set me up for emotional failure. I became such a slave to ensuring everyone else's outcomes that I didn't realize I was compliant in my own demise. I was petrified of being further ostracized if I complained. I learned not to defend myself, to suppress what I really felt, and to simply move on to the next thing. I understood and believed that I had no rights and no boundaries, and I got acquainted with being discriminated against, forgotten, overlooked, and threatened. There was no situation where I didn't recognize I was at a disadvantage. Every hill was an uphill climb with no boots. My self-worth was reduced to gratitude. I was supposed to be grateful for the crumbs from the master's table. Grateful in whatever situation I was in. Grateful to be living in Nana and Caroline's house. Grateful to have a relationship with my father. Grateful to have the jobs I rightfully earned. Grateful and undeserving. I was on my own, I turned the shit into fertilizer and used the isolation to forge ahead.

PART II: TERMS AND CONDITIONS

7

The Bank Teller

W*hew*! Who knew the "glass ceiling" was made of concrete and paved with White men and women and nepotism? I started my journey with bright eyes, an optimistic step, and a lot of hope that would propel me for years to come.

At seventeen, I started my banking career as a part-time teller. I worked twenty hours per week at $4.33 an hour on Wall Street. That may not sound like a lot, but the prestige of this position meant everything to this Black girl from the projects of Harlem. I was so excited to work in the bank. I'd always loved and excelled in school, and I knew that it was my high math aptitude and reasoning ability that landed me this coveted position as a (person of color) bank teller. I scored extremely high on the interview exam test. In the 1970s, you actually had to take an exam to get hired anywhere. It was nothing like nowadays when your gift of gab gets you the job—until the employer later discovers you can only write and speak in phonics, and can only do math with a computer.

My first day on the job was a moment in time that went slow like the speed of years but felt immense. The noisy hustle and bustle of the busy New York City streets, loud sounds, and the horns of Yellow Cabs blowing waned in the background of my existence as I stood in the lobby breathing in the essence of my reality. All those days of dreaming about being out of Nana's house felt like a tangible reality.

Except, I didn't just escape; I made it. I knew I walked into something like a dream come true. I had the results of my dreams laid out for many years. I wanted to buy my own clothes and be free from social workers telling me what I could and couldn't enjoy because of welfare, and I knew I wanted one of those high-rise apartments I'd dreamed about at Darryl's house.

Standing there, breathing in that crisp lobby air that smelled of highly polished wood, made me believe this was the way. Being a Black woman on the front lines of a bank was unheard of; after all, it had only been two years since women had earned the right to even get credit in their own name without a man. The enormity of this opportunity was not lost on me. I experienced the deep intersection of hope and the possibility that this was the way I would see everything I ever dreamed of. I stood in that grand lobby and stared in awe as my heart accepted the amazing opportunity before me. I took it all in.

The details of the enormous building gave me something more to hope for. Deep, rich mahogany wood-paneled walls and columns stood boldly to support its four-story ceiling. This massive beauty sat on all four corners of the New York City block. Its main entrance was located directly across the street from the New York Stock Exchange. Entering through the main entrance, up a flight of four steps, the lobby opened up in all of its opulence. White marble floors spread out before me, and beautiful crystal chandeliers above graced the enormous four-story high lobby. On my left was an elevator bank of six set off behind three massive wood columns. On my right were three separate customer areas: one for investment customers, one for businesses and elite customers with large balances—this area is where the Branch Manager (always a White man never visible or available to customers without an appointment) had his office and private bathroom behind a wood-paneled wall. From the outside, it looked like a big wooden box. The last area was for individuals. Straight ahead was the Teller's area —-twelve Teller stations flanked by the Operations area or "bond cage" and the Customer Service desk that led to the platform for individuals. It was massive and overwhelming. I had only ever seen the inside of a bank on the television show, *The Beverly Hillbillies*. I felt as if I was right in the middle of a fairytale to be working at this prestigious Wall Street bank. It was mind-blowing to think I was hired to work as a part of such a fine establishment.

Fashion wasn't for me like this moment was. I *belonged* here. I eventually dropped out of the Fashion Institute of Technology.

Finally, I was a professional. I was one of two Black people working on the banking floor (me behind the Tellers' area and Celeste on the platform). Black people mainly worked upstairs in the back office doing custodial, administrative, or data entry jobs. They were behind the scenes, never to be seen or heard, but that wasn't my story. I was hired to be front and center. As the stars would have it, my Teller's window was dead center, facing the entrance door. I was the first person a customer saw when they came into the bank. I wasn't preparing a runway walk anymore, but you couldn't tell me that didn't make me feel like I wasn't the star of the show.

I made it my business to own my excitement to be working in a professional environment. I have worked since I was thirteen years old when my main motivation was to never be dependent on welfare or any social handouts and to help my mother get some of the things she sacrificed for us. My focus now was looking ahead to what was to come.

Things began to progress for me. This job quickly evolved into a career. I was asked to come on full time, and I just wanted to make money and earn my right to climb the corporate ladder. I purchased my first two suits with my first paycheck of $65.00. One suit was gray and the other was beige. Each one cost me $19.99. I was so proud of myself and loved wearing my suits to work. I changed my blouses daily and enjoyed mixing and matching my outfits. Although I didn't share my excitement with Gordon, or anyone for that matter (as I was accustomed, still holding my feelings within), I was proud of myself more and more each day as I got dressed in one of my suits in our one-bedroom apartment.

My quest to know more led the way in my mastery of day-to-day bank operations. There were no ATMs back then. Facsimile (fax) machines were our main source of communication and technology. There were no emails, cell phones, or text messages. One phone was on the Supervisor's desk and only to be used in extreme emergencies or to communicate with other departments in the bank. Very few people were allowed to use the fax machine. We would take our documents to the Operation's area (cage) where faxes, wire transfers, and bonds were executed. The cage staff would set our documents up on the fax machine and then bring the document back to us with a receipt that it was sent.

I led my peers in proving (manually balancing) my cash box at the end of the day. We counted every dollar in our cash box by hand, and we Tellers would race to see who could finish fastest so we could help with the overall balancing of the branch. Doing these extra chores gave us opportunities for promotions.

I looked forward to whatever new thing was ahead of me at work. I went to work every day eager to learn and excel at something new. I soaked up everything. I was always looking, inquiring, and seeking out how to perform new skills and understand new concepts, especially the jobs that would help me grow. I meditated heavily on how I could do more to get promoted and eventually make $25,000 a year. I helped my Teller Supervisor, Mary, with the weekly cash shipments, which were all cash and

33

generally more than a million dollars, also to be counted by hand. I did all I could to earn the eyes for promotional opportunities. I helped train new Tellers, balanced the savings machines, and volunteered for a host of other responsibilities.

No matter what I did, Mary never encouraged or complimented me. She spent her time coaching and encouraging the White girls at the Tellers' line. Because I was accustomed to being shunned from my childhood experiences, I just kept on pushing myself to learn and lead. I never thought Nana and Caroline would be responsible for teaching me a transferable skill, but there I was, completely prepared to "be a big girl." Except this time, I knew my hard work wouldn't go unnoticed. No matter who Mary paid attention to, I made sure I was ready to meet the moment when it came.

Along with going the extra mile, I learned what to expect as normal in my new role. Every Friday was payday, and the lines would form from the Teller's window to the front door (the full length of the bank's city block). On Friday, we only had fifteen minutes for lunch, which we used to run into the break room to use the bathroom, smoke a cigarette, and then back to the Teller's window. No time for food. Truth be told, at our age we didn't even think about food. We worked nonstop from 9:00 a.m. to 5:00 p.m. and then went out for drinks at the end of the day to laugh and compare who had the craziest customer that day. We looked forward to it. We thrived on it.

At this point, my best friends at work were Susan and Sherrie, who were German and Italian. I loved being around people from different cultures. We learned a lot about each other's way of living and seeing the world mostly through osmosis because we didn't ask each other or care what our differences were. We simply accepted each other for who we were. The innocence of not understanding the prejudices of the world fueled our connectivity. We were just having fun and planning our next steps in life. We even defied the workplace norms and shared how much our raises were. *We didn't know we weren't "supposed" to.* We were over the moon for the extra twenty-five cents an hour and a $1,000 bonus twice a year. I couldn't wait to go home and share with Gordon when I got a raise. We counted every plateau. I was laser-focused on my target goal of earning $25,000 a year, and I was going to work as hard as I had to to get there.

I've always been an observer of people's behavior and am blessed enough to have the ability to adapt in the moment—build the plane while flying the plane—so to speak. The first thing I observed was how our cultural differences impacted our lives. While our conversations and fun times were very cohesive, culturally, we had different goals and very different ways of accomplishing them. We were all just struggling to figure out in our different ways how to achieve the American Dream that everyone talked about. Our conversations were filled with getting a raise, getting married, and having a family. Susan was already married and was trying hard to get pregnant. She wanted a baby so badly. *Good for her.* I knew then that Brandi would be an only child. Sherrie's entire focus was to get married, and it had to be before she was twenty-five. She was constantly speed-dating guys and giving them a two-month window. If they were not talking about short-term marriage goals and future family plans, she dumped them and moved on to the next. She eventually found her match, Donald, who turned out to be a very nice guy. We were all invited to their wedding. Gordon and I were the only Black people at this huge Italian wedding on Staten Island.

I started thinking that if Sherrie and I were both Tellers and made about the same amount of money, I could also have a ginormous wedding like this with all the frills. My thoughts muddled down the path of what else I could have, too. This inspirational moment sparked the light of possibility in me. It served its purpose until I found out that Sherrie had a lot of support at home. She later said her uncle helped a lot with her wedding expenses. I didn't have an uncle to help me, but that didn't dampen my spirits. Nothing would. I had already set my mind to it.

Meanwhile, Gordon and I shuffled Brandi on the train and bus between both of our mothers' apartments while we worked. We had no cell phones back then. Even if there was such a thing as a cell phone, I'm sure we would not have been able to afford one, let alone two or three. My sister would meet Brandi at the bus and call me at work once she got her to say she was there and okay. One of us would then pick her up after work and go home. I don't remember ever thinking something bad would happen. I think we were too young, or too broke, or both to consider the consequences. No one had a car to pick her up anyway. We just did what we had to do. Thank God we had no incidents.

Many people can never imagine their six-year-old riding the train or bus alone. Fortunately, Brandi always listened and was unusually smart. She recited the Gettysburg address with Gordon's aunt when she was just three years old. At the end of each day, I would make dinner, and we would always sit and eat together and discuss our day. It was one of my dreams and always important to me that we sat together, as a family, for at least one meal during the day to catch up on the day's events.

With shock and awe, Brandi now tells her children how, at six years old, she had to ride the train and bus alone from school to her grandmother's house. My grandkids listen and look wide-eyed at me with the unasked question of how I could have done such a horrible thing to their mother. I just laugh at them. These kids will never understand struggling. They are driven everywhere, and I think someone even chews their food for them before they swallow it.

Gordon and I lived together for three years before we got married. I already knew where I would have the wedding reception. Daddy drove us around, trying to convince me to look at other venues, but there was truly no need. I had already done my due diligence to dream of this moment and prepare for it. You would think I was paid to review venues by the level of commitment I had to scour bridal magazines. There was none like Le Cordon Bleu for me, and not a dime or person in the world could convince me otherwise. No amount of driving around was going to change my mind. Finally, Daddy informed Gordon, "We are just wasting our time." Daddy knew me better than anyone, and he knew my mind was already settled. Perhaps my certainty zapped the fun of the process because I knew the precise wedding gown I wanted, too. I knew my wedding gown would be an "Eve of Milady" gown, and once everyone else got on board with my preset vision, the wedding bells started ringing. Ironically, Mommy didn't come with me to get my dress—Lilly did. I paid for it and also bought outfits for everyone in my family to wear to the wedding.

Gordon and I had the big, ginormous wedding I knew we could have. We had a wedding party of fourteen attendants and over one hundred fifty guests at $30.00 per plate and all the glitz and glam that went with it. We had no "uncle" to help–Daddy threw in $1,000–and with lots of planning, budgeting, and focusing on the goal (my specialty), we had the wedding of my dreams.

I had never seen a dream of mine come together so clearly and harmoniously. Every detail set the magical stage for an unforgettable pause in time. The glow and glisten of my dress made up for the "oohs" and "ahhs" I missed from prom. The atmosphere was ripe with smiles and laughter, and love and praise filled the room. We kissed and danced the night away as our loved ones ate to their hearts' content and joined in our celebration. All the right characters were in place, and they didn't fail to leave their personalities behind.

We were the first of our families and neighborhood friends to have this kind of wedding. Gordon and I were the talk of the neighborhood—and not always in a good way. They were proud of us, but that did not stop the gossipers from speculating. There were stories about how we were still paying for our wedding long after the wedding was over. The gossip kept spreading, and the lies kept compounding. People had a hard time accepting that we were determined to be different, so rumors were the easiest to digest. The rumors gave us a good laugh to shrug off every time they circled back to us.

Their speculations proved that they were clueless about how this works, as if the reception hall was going to let us have a wedding without paying in full before the event. Despite the rumors, they were happy to be on the guest list. It was such a big deal that we even had some wedding crashers who were not on the list. We just let them in, found a seat for them, and made it work. It was such a night to remember for more than just Gordon and me. It was a defining moment for both our families and communities. We were breaking the mold of the environments we came from. It may have appeared to some that we had a whole lot of money to blow, but the truth was that we spent our last on that wedding.

We were so freaking broke after the reception, we sent Brandi home with her grandmother and after seeing our last guests off, we took a taxi home. We didn't even have money to pay the fare. We were in the back seat of the taxi, drunk, laughing hysterically, and tearing open envelopes, hoping to find enough cash to pay before we reached the house. In between spinning around dizzily in the back seat, and laughing until we couldn't breathe, we'd yell out, "I found a five!" "I found a ten!" Gordon finally opened an envelope with two twenties. *The size of the gifts was reflective of the economic and social status of us and our guests in the 80's.* Gordon and I threw our hands up in praise as we burst out, toppled over with laughter and a missed high-five. That moment turned into a hug. Our drunken confidence turned into a math moment. Now with more than enough to cover the taxi ride, we had the driver stop at the store, and we bought some snacks to take home with us. Our night came to a close, but our world was opening to new horizons.

Life after getting married was great, but we only got a little time together before our family dynamic shifted. Gordon was an only child and his mother moved in with us shortly after we got married. She said she felt alone and like she was losing her only baby—as if she weren't aware that one day he would get older and have his own family.

Having my mother-in-law living with us as newlyweds was a double-edged sword, but at least I got a live-in babysitter out of the deal. No more shuffling Brandi through the city. This made for four of us living in our one-bedroom apartment. I was young, so the overcrowding didn't bother me like it should have. It was bumpy settling in as anyone can imagine living with any in-law, especially a mother-in-law. She would get up at the crack of dawn so she could beat me to the kitchen to fix Gordon's breakfast. I eased her mind and told her she didn't have anything to worry about. I was never going to get up early to fix his breakfast. That settled it. She got up and fixed breakfast for all of us and even had dinner prepared when we got home. Problem solved. I love removing obstacles for people so they can live their best life. It was a great arrangement. Besides, Gordon and I had our careers to focus on.

Gordon had worked at his job in a public relations firm for ten years. They were downsizing, and Gordon started getting a lot of pressure at work. Gordon did not like change. He was the type of guy who was really good when things were predictable, but he spiraled with bad anxiety when he didn't know what was next. The stress caused him to have really bad nose bleeds almost every day. I finally told him to just quit and find something else. We would be okay until he got another job. He was so shocked that I was willing to carry our family until he found another job. It was a no-brainer for me. Our vows said for better or worse. I carried us when he couldn't and vice versa. That is what I believe a partnership is about.

In the interim, Gordon applied at the phone company; fortunately for us, a few weeks after he quit the public relations firm, the phone company hired him. Thank God. We now had a job with security *and* benefits. Back then, the phone company not only had the best benefits package around, but the benefits were also free to its employees and families, and you almost had to commit an act of God to be terminated. When you were hired by the phone company, it was automatically assumed that you would work there until you retired. Gordon was happily following in his mother's footsteps, who had also retired from the phone company.

Life wasn't perfect, but I was well on my way to living out the next dream of success I had in my heart. The projects were distant enough that I had them in the rearview, but my American Dream of living in the high-rise apartments was still far enough away that more work had to be done. The journey was motivation because we were finally moving and grooving at a good pace, and stability tasted within reach. Gordon and I were both fully and gainfully employed, and we had benefits and were able to experience some of the luxuries welfare would have said we shouldn't have. Our little family was complete. With things stabilizing in my personal life, I shifted all my attention to my career.

The bank eventually hired another Black Teller. That made three Black people on the banking floor. Henrietta, who was from Belize, had just come to the United States and quickly became my very best work friend and confidante. Henrietta was five years older than me and taught me many ways to cope with the discrimination I suffered from Mary. She would always encourage me to just ignore Mary. Sherrie and Susan would just look at me sheepishly and smile and love on me more when we went out after for drinks. I don't think they knew any more than I did how to handle discrimination. Although Black, Henrietta was immediately accepted since she had an accent and was not a Black American. I had always wanted to feel special, but certainly not in this bizarre way.

An Error Resolution

I worked so hard to earn what I thought was my way up through the ranks. I tried to learn everything I needed to know so that if an opportunity became available, I would be a shoo-in. I would get the position based on my work ethic and experience. However, while I was working my butt off believing that hard work would yield positive rewards, things didn't happen like that at all. I worked my way around the Teller's area and learned everything there was to know. However, my goal was to work on the platform as a bank Customer Service Officer.

When a position became available, Mary went to the Branch Manager and told him to "take Henrietta because she will be really good over there." Mary knew that this was what I worked hard for; everyone knew. But whatever her reason, Mary adored Henrietta. Mary never raised my name for the position or considered my work ethic and accomplishments. That was the first slap in my face in the workplace. My first experience of work discrimination. In my naivete, I still did not understand what happened or was able to put a label on it. Mary knew that I could do the work, and I knew it, too—everyone did. I tried to give Mary the benefit of the doubt. I just concluded that she was holding me back to avoid having to train someone else to do the extra work in the Teller's area. Perhaps she wanted me to stay on her team because I was an asset. I knew she wasn't interested in training someone else to do the extra work in the Teller's area, and I had mastered it. The more I tried to extend this grace, the more Mary's behaviors taught me to accept who she really was.

Celeste was the Black Officer who worked on the platform when I was hired and was probably about ten years older than me. I felt supported without her ever having to express it. We did not talk often, but I always felt she was watching over me like I imagined a big sister would. She never told me what to do but occasionally gave me tidbits of wisdom about how to navigate the waters of banking. Although she was not in a powerful position to be a forerunner for me, I felt that she quietly had my back.

It was rare that Celeste and I had a break at the same time. This particular day we were in the break room together when she said her husband was thinking of moving out of state, and she would have to sell her house. I just blurted out, "If you sell your house, let me know." I quickly rambled on about nothing at this point because I didn't know what made me say that. My quick thinking caused me to take quick action before I could rationalize what I had just gotten myself into. I guess I thought because she was Black, worked at the bank, and if she had a house, I could probably get a house too.

Three weeks later, Celeste came to me and said, "Were you serious about buying my house? Because we are moving."

Without any hesitation, I said, "Yes." I had not even spoken to Gordon, *clueless about what buying a house entailed,* but I somehow knew that this was an opportunity of a lifetime. Fortunately, Gordon trusted me and was always supportive of my goals and dreams even when they were from left field. It was obvious we were beyond our space limits in the one bedroom, and I was sure I would get his support on this, but his support was the furthest thing from my mind. My only thought was how I actually have an opportunity to own a home. Homeownership was not even on my radar.

Truth be told, our cramped surroundings would have only led me to look for a larger apartment, maybe one with the river view of my dreams, but I never dreamed of buying a house. When I went home and told him, he said, "Darlene!, how are we going to buy a house?"

I said, "If we can pay rent, we should be able to pay a mortgage." I could see his wheels were spinning. He could not deny the rationale that I once again blurted out, but that triggered his emotions about change. Paying rent was safe and familiar for Gordon. We had done the unimaginable with the wedding, and I knew we could do it again. A mortgage was much harder to fathom as a reality. Only in Hollywood did Black people in the '80s "move on up" to the proverbial "east side" and own homes. His fear of the unknown was valid, but he could not deny that we desperately needed more space, and the same money we earned to pay the rent would be spent on a mortgage. He reluctantly muttered out his agreement, but I knew he was one foot in and one foot out in heart. I had no idea how we could afford to buy a house or what it entailed, but again, if my co-workers could do it on their salaries, then we should be able to do it on ours.

In 1983, mortgage rates at sixteen percent on average were irrelevant to me. I just believed if we could pay monthly rent, then we could pay a monthly mortgage, and we could afford the house. My going philosophy was that I didn't have enough money to be concerned with rates. Cash was still king" and if you could earn it and pay your bills, you could achieve it. Everything else was just obstacles to overcome. With the new women's right to have credit in their name, my income would also be considered when we applied for a mortgage. Back then, you only needed a letter of verification of employment to get approved. I had reached my $25,000-a-year salary goal, so I knew with both our salaries, we had the income.

My Branch Manager wrote a letter to confirm my employment and salary and that I had access to funds in my 401(k) plan that I could use as a down payment. Gordon did the same at his company. I was twenty-four, and we bought our first house for $52,000. All of those nights of dreaming about being out of Nana's house; all those days of wanting a place to call my own; every moment I spent dreaming at Darryl's house in that high-rise apartment; and a host of other thoughts and emotions were swirling around my head all at once. We *really* purchased a home. It. Was. Ours. Nobody could take it away from us. Excitement paled in comparison to the joy I experienced. I wasn't too worried about the next steps because it all felt really, *really* good.

Gordon couldn't believe we had actually bought a house, and he was very hesitant that we would be able to keep it. Who was I fooling? I couldn't believe it either; but unlike Gordon, I had no doubts we wouldn't keep it.

Gordon spent the first day of every month after we paid the mortgage saying, "Well, I can say I owned a house for a month;" "I can say I owned a house for two months;" and he would say this every month for the first year we lived there. It wasn't always easy making that mortgage payment. Some months we had to decide if we were going to pay Brandi's Catholic school tuition or mortgage. Some bills went in the proverbial hat, and some didn't make it to the hat. If all else failed, I was determined that Brandi was going to have a great education, and we were going to have a roof over our heads.

Other than Daddy, his two brothers, and Gordon's aunt, we didn't know anyone else who had ever owned a house, but we made the most of the experience. We hosted summer barbecues, celebrated friends' birthdays, and by default hosted Thanksgiving dinner every year because Gordon and Brandi always complained about other people's food. If we went to someone's house for Thanksgiving, they would start complaining even before we left home because I was not cooking food at home for them to eat when we returned.

Once we arrived, they would start making inquiries to me about the food. It was embarrassing. They would ask me—not so discreetly either—who made the potato salad, who made the dressing, on and on through each dish. I decided it was easier for me to just cook at home and have everyone over to our house.

One weekend, Brandi spent the night at her aunt's and told her I only eat my mother's eggs." When she brought her back home, earlier than planned, my sister-in-law was so distraught, saying that Brandi had not eaten anything at her house the whole weekend. After she left, I asked Brandi what happened, and she said, "Mommy when you cook chicken, I see you washing it in the sink. Auntie just took the chicken out of the pack and put it in the pot." That's my girl, always watching people.

In my own overprotectiveness, it was fine. I never wanted Brandi to spend the night at anyone's house anyway. It was okay for them to come to ours, but I didn't trust people to take care of her the way I did. Plus, you never knew what people would do in their homes. I just couldn't imagine putting Brandi in a situation where she could potentially be victimized.

Someone once said to me, "Brandi is like your pocketbook; you take her everywhere you go."

I said, "Yes; if she's not welcome, I don't go."

8
Major Deductions and Hidden Fees

'd always believed I could do and obtain anything anyone else could. I only had to decide what I wanted, and nothing would stop me from believing I could have it. All I had to do was work hard and make it happen.

My strategy was simple. Who could deny hard work? After all, how hard could hard really be? Not easy for a Black woman in the banking industry, and it took me my entire career to realize that. The first leg of my career was with that aesthetically beautiful bank on Wall Street in New York City across the street from the New York Stock Exchange. I gained so much knowledge and experience during my time there. After I'd been there ten years, they closed their retail branches. We were given the option of going to one of the savings banks that were acquiring our retail accounts or taking a severance package. I opted for the severance package.

As we grew our families and careers, Sherrie, Susan, and I eventually drifted apart. However, forty-five years later, Henrietta and I are still very good friends. She has since retired and moved back to Belize. Our birthdays are a week apart, and we call each other every year and just pick up right where we left off.

My decision to accept the severance package was pivotal to the rest of my career, and it took me on a journey I could not have imagined. The money came at a perfect time since Brandi was graduating from high school and I was adamant she went to college.

I did not want to be hypocritical. I also returned to school and finished my Bachelors. Returning to school reminded me of how much I'd always enjoyed it, and I quickly discovered how much I also enjoyed community service. I started volunteering around the city.

This was a great time in my life—even with the blip of a very painful, six-week ectopic pregnancy. I loved being on the cutting edge of change that helped others. I graduated with honors, was named student liaison to my alumni association, and was chairperson of the commencement ceremony. I also worked in the school's grants and development office between classes.

My supervisor, Jane, was such a hard worker, very insightful, and a realist. I worked beside her tirelessly and sometimes late into the night. She taught me how to write, edit, and apply for grants for the school's science and math departments, but she also taught me something about how the White world (really her world) works. She showed me how positioning yourself for success works for them.

Jane had two kids who were going off to college. One day she and I were chatting about life, and Jane said, "My daughter isn't the brightest kid but she's pretty, so she will have to get into college and meet a professor and get him to marry her to secure her future." Mentally, I froze, and I'm sure my whole face and body would have communicated the shock had it not been for my learned stoicism. *Did she really just say that?* I couldn't believe what my ears had just heard. Appalled was an understatement. Did she *really* believe the best her daughter could do in this life was to be pretty? Jane was smart and insightful and had taught me so much in such a short time. *Surely* she could teach her daughter to be more than just pretty.

I didn't understand the underlying message Jane was communicating then. I later came into my own understanding of connections and power in our society. I had to learn that most people were willing to do anything to get it. I was too young and too culturally unaware to really understand the power play she was describing. Had I known how to take advantage of the position I was in to develop the skills she was sharing, I could have learned how to make some power plays of my own.

Jane came to me shortly before I graduated with a newspaper article and said, "Look! Darlene! Cornell University is looking for twenty students for this program. Darlene, you should apply. I know you can get one of them."
I said, "Jane, they're only offering twenty spots."

She was persistent. "I know, and you can definitely win one of these seats. You only need to write an essay."

I wasn't so sure about applying. Cornell was a prestigious Ivy League university, and it's not like it was open to everyone who applied. Other than my father and Gordon, I was new to the experience of someone else believing in me, so I moved forward with a lot of reluctance. Plus, Gordon had been carrying all of the expenses—without ever complaining. He always said, "Shit, I don't care if you never go back to work. As long as you're happy and we have a roof over our heads and food to eat, you can do whatever you want." I loved him for that. I still felt I should go back to work. I wrote my essay, completed my application, submitted it, and started looking for work.

Cornell responded and invited me to be one of the twenty students to attend their Master of Science in Labor Relations program that year. I was blown away. Another opportunity presented to me unexpectedly, just like when we bought the house. I had made it to the big leagues, and I wasn't even trying!

I had so many goals before me, but I never dreamt of continuing my education beyond my bachelor's degree, much less attending an Ivy League school. I was elated, and my plate was full while embarking on this new and unexpected educational opportunity. My classes at Cornell were held downstate at Baruch College in the city, which allowed me to go back to work full-time while earning my degree.

I got a job as an assistant to the Director of the Transportation Research Center at The City College of New York (CUNY). We were a consortium of twelve universities and did various types of research to improve transportation and energy sources in the region. Some of the initiatives we worked on included helping to develop New York City's Metro card, the tram from Manhattan to the John F. Kennedy airport, the Second Avenue subway line (which is still on the table to be built), and how to use rubber tires among other sources for energy.

I constantly explored ways to be promoted. I aimed to work my way from being the Assistant to the Director to being the Assistant Director of the Research Center. Once promoted to Assistant Director, I developed the first marketing tool (a catalog of white papers) to generate revenue for the Center and I was appointed Editor of the Center's newsletter. By establishing research partners within the community, I increased its distribution by two hundred percent. I also earned a certificate in how to facilitate adult training and development. This job served as a great training platform for my future leadership roles in banking.

While I was thriving in school and in my new role, many other things were going on in my personal life. Some days, it was hard to keep up with it all. Brandi was off to college, and my marriage to Gordon was quickly disintegrating. It had become clear we wanted different things and our visions of the future were not the same.

For two years, I would leave work at five, jump in my car, and race downtown through New York City's rush hour traffic to get to class. I had to arrive at just the right time as the other classes were ending in order to grab one of the coveted midtown Manhattan parking spaces and still be in class by six. When class ended at eight, I was back in the car driving home to Queens to cook dinner for Gordon and me.

I watched him sit in his beach chair in the middle of our living room having his daily gin and coke while waiting for dinner. Gordon was a creature of habit. He put the *same* in *sameness*. He was a homebody who wanted the same thing, every time, in the same way.

Living with Gordon was like watching a robot set on autopilot. His daily routine was to come home from work, change clothes, fix his gin and coke, sit in his beach chair in front of the television watching the news, then *Jeopardy* and *Wheel of Fortune,* while waiting for me to call him to dinner. On the weekends he hung out with his friends in Harlem.

I was the total opposite. I was bursting at the seams, hardly able to sit still, wanting to explore and learn everything. My brand-new world as an "empty-nester" was full of possibility and opportunity, and I was so excited to dig in at every chance I could. I was hungry for more, new, and the unfamiliar, and Gordon couldn't be further from it.

Despite our meager beginnings, we had successfully raised Brandi, survived the exorbitant cost of a Catholic school education, got her off to college, and set her up for a successful future. We were even able to buy Brandi a car. A big red clunker. I'm sure it was the biggest car on campus, but she was surrounded by steel and was safe. I had a partner and a house, and the world was my oyster. All I could do was dream about what was next for me—for us.

For three years after Brandi went to college, I stuck it out with Gordon. I tried to find a way we could align our visions. I wanted us to go on dates, go for walks in Central Park, travel, and whatever else came our way. I looked for ways we could connect but to no avail. I finally asked Gordon what he wanted.

He said, "I figured we would just sit and chill and wait for Brandi to have babies and help her raise her kids." It felt like a jolt, as if someone had slammed on the emergency brakes while I was going ninety miles an hour.

"*What?* She just went to college! Are you seriously planning to just come home every day, sit in your beach chair with your gin and coke, wait for Brandi to finish college, meet a man, get married, and have children before you do anything else?" I was outraged. This was absurd to me, and he was only surprised that I was surprised. As if, how could life be any other way?

I said, "I'm not waiting for Brandi to graduate college to live my life, and I am *definitely*!! not going to help her raise her kids." I said it with so much defiance because letting those words escape my mouth gave me the permission I needed to exit stage right. It was clear that no matter how hard we tried, our boats were simply not rowing in the same direction. The slam on the brakes that occurred in this conversation taught me everything that I needed to know about the hard stop in life that was coming. I could no longer deny we were headed to separate destinations, and it was only a matter of time before one of us had to jump ship.

Communication proved so important to me in that moment. Had we never had that conversation, we would still be trying to row this marriage boat in two different directions. He was fine with being an anchor, and I needed to sail the seas of possibility. We were co-existing with very different thoughts about our future, and seeing us "together" became a bleak imagination.

I felt guilty initiating the separation because Gordon had always supported me through all my dreams and desires. He was supportive of my goals while I went back to school full-time to complete both my bachelor's and master's degrees. I had also promised his mother, on her deathbed, that I would never leave him alone. It felt so unfair to leave him on the heels of obtaining my master's degree.

It felt like I was abandoning him, but I was suffocating under the guise of safety and monotony. Growth and exploration were a lifeline to me. Venturing down the roads of the unknown path to get to some desired end was the fuel in my blood, and I could not breathe under the weight of settling, rote consistency, and predictable routines. It wasn't safe for me. I thrived in figuring it out. I knew that so many of my hopes would die if I tried to stay in this safe, predictable plateau of expectations he called life. I knew I would die right along with my hopes and dreams in that house, and perishing simply wasn't an option. We had come so far, or at least I thought we had, but he wanted to stop going. I decided I wanted to keep living, and that was when I decided to transition. It was time.

Of course, Daddy, my biggest fan and always my protector, came to see me. Just as he spent days driving me around to find the wedding venue of my dreams, he came to me and spent hours having an in-depth conversation with me about whether my wanting a divorce after sixteen years was the right thing for me. Daddy was my sounding board and my confidant. We always had open, honest conversations about my feelings, my well-being, and the impact of my decisions, and this conversation was no different.

Against Gordon's wishes, after sixteen years of marriage, we decided to separate and sell our home. I helped him find and furnish his new apartment in Harlem—Gordon always said he wanted to live and die in Harlem. I found and furnished my new apartment. I stayed in Queens— suburbia was definitely my thing. Neither of us ran off to file for divorce since neither of us had anyone waiting in the wings. We had simply just grown apart. We still loved each other and remained really good friends.

Being by myself after all of those years, and for the first time, was eerie. The first year was quiet, almost too quiet at times. I cried many nights in that apartment, questioning if I had done the right thing by leaving Gordon. After all, hadn't I achieved the proverbial American Dream? *Why wasn't it enough for me?*

The walls had never become more interesting, and I was excited about any opportunity to not sit still and focus on the fact that I was alone. I welcomed all the distractions. I did all the things to keep me busy as I navigated this new season in life. It took me some time, but it suddenly dawned on me that I had the green light to go after everything I wanted without hindrance, so that's what I did.

After earning my master's degree, I still worked at the Research Center and was unsure of what I would do next. A former colleague called and asked if I was interested in working in an investment firm part-time in the evenings. At first, I said no, but thought, what else would I be doing in the evenings? I studied and earned my New York Series 6 and 63 investment licenses. I started working part-time three evenings a week.

You never know what path a detour will take you. It was these licenses that got the attention of a headhunter for a bank. A recruiter called me and asked if I would consider managing a branch they had acquired in Harlem. Banks had started evolving with technology. Gone were the wooden columns and high ceilings with the Branch Manager's office in the middle of the platform. Everything in banks was now metal, sleek, and high-tech, and the Branch Manager now only had a desk, front and center, with access from all employees and customers. I was offered $60,000 a year and the title of Vice President with the condition to earn my Series 7 investment license within a year. I excitedly accepted.

I would be lying if I didn't say I was excited; however, looking back, the horror of it all was that I was only offered $60,000 a year.

How ironic is this? In twenty-two years I went full circle, from mother, wife, bank Teller, homeowner, and student, to earning two degrees, back to being single, back into banking to become Vice President and Branch Manager, and back home to Harlem. God's plans for me were definitely higher than any I could have ever imagined for myself. I started traveling regularly. I spent my days on the beach in the Bahamas studying for my Series 7 license and my nights partying at the many clubs in the Bahamas. I obtained my Series 7 license within three months of starting my new job at the bank.

Having been born and raised in Harlem, I was accepted into the community with open arms. This acceptance was a natural alliance with my innate passion for wanting to make a positive difference in the lives of the people I touched. This bank had always been known for its commercial business and never in "impoverished" communities. Acquiring the dying breed of the savings and loan banks was an opportunity for them to change their strategy. I was a great hire for them—a Black person born in and who knows the community—and they were a great re-entry for me back into the banking industry, this time with more credentials and leadership experience.

A part of the bank's acquisition agreement was that all salary increases and promotions be frozen for the first year. I was able to maintain a zero-level turnover rate while I motivated my team to stay on board until the freeze was lifted. Staying on during that year positioned them to be given the first opportunity for all job openings when the freeze was lifted and to receive their earned bonuses and salary increases.

During that year, we increased the branch's revenue by twenty-three and a half percent. I collaborated with the bank's Community Development Team to ensure activities were in place to maintain positive ratings under the government's Community Reinvestment Act. We were thriving and everyone loved what I was doing for the bank in the Harlem community. Well, that is everyone except my immediate manager, Catherine.

She was a strange bird. She would have us managers come to her office for our monthly review. I'd walk into her office, and immediately facing me was this huge wooden cross on the dingy, yellowing wall over her head. She was always drably dressed in long dresses with colors of olive greens and tans, and she had dirty-looking, oily blonde hair plastered to the sides of her head like a helmet. It immediately disarmed me because each time I felt like I was walking into what I imagined a convent would be like, and then she'd open her mouth and say something contrary and evil, even slanderous. She once told me she was not impressed with nor did she care about my successes because she thought I was a lazy slug. Thinking back, I wonder if her calling me a "slug" was her covert way of calling me the "N" word, especially since I was anything but lazy. *Hmmm.*

For some reason, I was always the bane of existence for my White female managers.

I had so much love and support around me while making a positive impact on our region that I didn't even take heed to what she said. I just did a Mabel Cooper (Mommy) on her—held my head high and ignored her. Her insults were like water off a duck's back. The more I succeeded, the more she appeared to dislike me. It may have been the one time in my career I was truly happy and not actively looking for the next promotion or the next best thing. It was nirvana for me.

Well, maybe not exactly true. Don't get me wrong, while I was not looking for a promotion, I would have gladly applied for Catherine's job if it was available. I am sure I could have led the team more positively than she did, and I certainly would not have been calling people slugs.

From Single to Joint Accounts

I was acclimating to being single, and my friend Cynthia, also single, and I were traveling often, enjoying the single girl's life. Realizing that individually we were spending a lot of money on rent and taxes, Cynthia and I decided it would be more beneficial for us to purchase a house together. We bought a four-bedroom house in New Jersey and did some major renovations to make it work for us. I took the two bedrooms and bathroom upstairs, and she took the two bedrooms and bathroom on the first floor, and we shared the common areas.

Unlike when I started in banking, got married, raising Brandi, struggling to pay my mortgage and Catholic school tuition, being a single woman and not quite forty was a different kind of experience altogether, one that I thoroughly enjoyed, and I vowed never to get married again. The freedom of doing anything I wanted without being responsible for anyone else was so heady and much deserved. It was also the time in my life I had hit my stride.

Everything was going well in business and my personal life. When I wasn't traveling, I was at Saks 5th Avenue, buying the best designer clothes and shoes. At six feet, two inches tall, I wore nothing less than three or four-inch heels every day, parking my brand-new car in the parking lot down the street from my office, and strutting down Seventh Avenue in Harlem, saying good morning to all the familiar faces, with my red suit and red leather slingback shoes on hot summer days, catching the attention of people wherever I went.

I spent my evenings and nights with friends at community meetings or bar hopping around Harlem, making connections and moves, and then driving home and enjoying homeownership for the second time. My God, I was having so much fun doing all of the things I enjoyed.

The community work I did while earning my bachelor's degree afforded me many outreach skills. I was able to use those skills to develop numerous partnerships in Harlem to help deliver the bank positively to the Harlem community. I used my adult training tools to help people in the community navigate the intricacies of basic banking by facilitating financial education seminars. I was recognized in and by the community for delivering financial education and programs to its members.

Additionally, I went into the middle schools to teach teens how to budget and balance a checkbook. I received special acknowledgment from parents and the political body for my contribution of school supplies to the local schools. I co-sponsored a forum with the local senator to help the community understand the impact of genocide on the Harlem community during its Renaissance. I chaired the Jackie Robinson Park Conservancy Board to keep one of the only two park bandshells left in Manhattan from being torn down. I also served as a director on the Harlem Hospital Community Advisory Board, where we met weekly to discuss how and why the hospital was viewed more as a scourge than an asset to the community. As a result, the city had planned to close the hospital. Having been born in Harlem Hospital, with family in the community and now working in the community, I was a huge stakeholder.

I, along with other community advocates and top administrators of the hospital, fought and built a case for why it was important for the hospital to stay and keep its doors open as a pillar in the community. We won and were instrumental in not just keeping its doors open, but we also developed a plan to increase its footprint and bring in the much-needed state-of-the-art technology.

One evening I was interviewed by the news in front of the hospital about my advocacy to keep Harlem Hospital open, and Gordon called and asked me if I was now going to be a politician. I cracked up laughing and said no, just doing what I can for my beloved Harlem.

This was just about the time I met Maurier. I remember so vividly the day he came into the bank. Maurier owned his own company and was looking for someone to help set up check-cashing privileges for his employees. Someone recommended that he come to see me. He was six feet, six inches tall, with great football shoulders out to everywhere making a definite presence when he walked into the bank. He had on a tee shirt that said something or another about Big Daddy.

The other girls and I were always teasing about guys who came into the bank, though I had always vowed never to date a customer or co-worker—and up to then I had not. When Maurier was walking out, I whispered to Jan, *Yes, I want him to be my big daddy.* We cracked up laughing. I honestly didn't think anything else of it.

Maurier was often coming into the bank to take care of business, and he actively pursued me. He asked me to go to dinner several times, but somehow our schedules didn't sync. I was always traveling. He said that every time he asked me to dinner, I was leaving for the Bahamas. He was right. Cynthia and I went to the Bahamas at least four times a year. We were both single and making good money, and back then airfare and hotel for seven days in the Bahamas was only about six hundred dollars.

One day, Maurier came into the bank and invited me and my entire staff to his birthday party. I did not go. Later, when we finally went to dinner and talked about his birthday invitation, I told him I don't party with my staff. He said the only reason he invited them was so that I would come, and I said the only reason I did not come was because you invited them. It made me think of the "Gift of the Magi." Our first date was so much fun. We laughed and talked about almost everything.

Two months into dating Maurier, Daddy died. Unfortunately, Maurier never got the chance to meet Daddy. I think he would have liked Maurier. They have the same family values and would do anything for their families. I always said that the world could not handle me having the love of two great men at the same time so, sadly, one of them had to go.

Daddy went into the hospital for a simple procedure. Gallstones, I think. I went to pick him and Lilly up, and we drove to the hospital. The procedure was a success and he went to recovery. We stayed with him for a bit, and then he told us to go home and get some rest.

The next day when we went to visit him, he had been moved to the ICU. There was no explanation for what happened to him other than he took a turn for the worse overnight. It was so unbelievable. His doctor was away for the weekend, the staff there couldn't seem to give us any straight answers, and the doctor on call wasn't responding. Things were so bad that Andre even came to visit him in the hospital. I remember Daddy saying to Andre, "I must be dying if you came to see me." We still couldn't grasp how serious things were. We stayed with him late into the night. Before we finally went home I asked Lilly if she would be going to church with me the next day. At first, she said no, and then she said okay.

I picked her up for church. It was Father's Day. For the life of me, the service went on and on forever. I believe they gave everyone at church and all the surrounding area a Father's Day award. And then out of nowhere, the sun lit up the entire church, and every stained glass window sparkled. The service was finally over, and Lilly and I went to the hospital. As we walked out of the parking garage, my Uncle Jimmy, Daddy's brother, was walking toward us. When he got to us, he said that Daddy was gone. I fell to the street. Sitting on the curb, I couldn't move. Lilly kept going. She started running into the hospital.

Uncle Jimmy said, "Darlene, don't worry. I'll be here for you. I'll take his place."

All I could say was, "You can't."

In retrospect, I sounded so cruel. And then out of nowhere, Brandi was there saying, "Mommy you don't have to do anything. I already went inside and identified Granddaddy." I just looked at her. Brandi, usually so emotional, had taken control of the situation, and just like that, I realized she had grown up.

I was surprised. Brandi, the only grandchild for the first fifteen years of her life, was very close to her grandfather, and I would have expected her to be the one to fall apart. Daddy's death almost broke me, but in my brokenness, Brandi had grown up. *My baby was grown.*

I chauffeured Lilly around while she made the arrangements for Daddy's funeral, but once my brother Grant arrived, she dumped me and ignored me as if I were never there. She then invited Uncle Jimmy to come over, and he and Grant divided Daddy's clothes. She never even asked if I wanted anything of his. I was hurt. I was devastated.

True to his word, my Uncle Jimmy was with me from that day forward. There was not a celebration or event that I had where Uncle Jimmy didn't show up for me. He was my rock.

After the day Daddy died, I went on autopilot, and I never cried in front of anyone again—until Uncle Jimmy's funeral twenty years later. Uncle Jimmy was loved by so many people. His funeral was standing room only, and people spilled out onto the streets to be there. I was sitting with Maurier. One minute I was okay, and the next it was like a dam had broken in me, and I made loud, heart-wrenching, guttural sobs. It felt like I was crying for every loss and every pain I had ever endured.

I kept telling myself to stop disrupting the service, to get it together, but my sobs were uncontrollable for more than ten minutes. I just kept wailing and wailing, barely able to catch my breath. Then as suddenly and as unexpectedly as they started, my sobs stopped. I felt like I had gone through a cleansing. I was depleted.

After Daddy died, Maurier and I continued to go out on dates. He talked about getting married often. In my mind, that was a big red flag because I had already vowed never to get married again. Single life was *waaay* too much fun. Having spent my youth being a responsible wife and mother, I wanted to travel and do all the things I missed out on. Maurier says he knew he wanted to marry me the day that he met me. I was thinking booty call.

The one thing I remember most about our dates is the laughter and the new experiences with different cuisines. He introduced me to cuisines I never knew existed. Maurier always made me laugh. We just had good, clean fun and built a strong friendship, and while mentally I kept saying I didn't want to get married again, I *almost* couldn't imagine having this much fun with someone else. Almost, because when we weren't hanging out, I was still single and enjoying my freedom and the single life very much. I had the best of both worlds.

Seven months later, Maurier and I went to the Poconos for my birthday. I just knew he was going to ask me to marry him. I just had that feeling, so on the drive back, I said, "If you are going to ask me to marry you, I don't want an engagement ring."

He said, "Well, alrighty then! Let's get married."

We started laughing. Always the dreamer and planner, the reason I didn't want an engagement ring was that I wanted a wedding band with a full circumference of diamonds—totally different from the gold band that Gordon designed for me. Later when we went to the jewelers to design my ring, Maurier said, "I think that it would have been cheaper for me to buy you an engagement ring." We both laughed.

The day after Maurier asked me to marry him, we were sitting in his car and reality hit me. I couldn't believe it. Seven years after Gordon and I separated I was actually planning to get married again. I guess I sobered from the giddiness of the proposal. I said to Maurier, "Before we get married, I have two questions to ask you. One, would we only be allowed to have missionary sex?"

He laughed and said, "Of course not." It may sound like a stupid question, but Maurier was also studying to become a deacon in his church, and while I went to church regularly, I was totally naive to the expected behavior of a wife of someone who served in a leadership capacity at church. In my experience, church people sometimes made everything seem like a sin.

My second question was to ask if he could take care of me. Not financially, but my well-being, take care of my heart. He said that he could. Funny that once he asked me to marry him, giving up my single life never occurred to me. It was not even a thought. Marrying Maurier seemed like the most obvious thing to do. He had worn me down without me ever realizing it. I think that is what love should be, just the next logical step. An obvious and unexpected occurrence.

I filed for divorce from Gordon and Maurier and I got married eight months later. I did not have all of the glitz and glam of my first wedding, but a small wedding—a party of six, less than a hundred guests at a rooftop ballroom in Maurier's hometown in Connecticut. With Daddy now deceased, Brandi gave me away. The priorities I had as a twenty-three-year-old bride were worlds apart from what they were for me as a forty-five-year-old bride.

My first dream of homeownership was a leap of faith. This time it was planned. Maurier and I were looking for somewhere to live in New Jersey, but the taxes were just too high, so we were forced to search in Pennsylvania. This was another unexpected blessing. As God would have it, we built our first custom home just a few miles away from where we stayed the weekend he asked me to marry him. It was a five thousand, two hundred square-foot, two-story colonial on a golf course with five bedrooms, four bathrooms, a finished basement, and a dream that almost didn't come true. We had to work hard to pull together the closing costs, emptying bank accounts and all our savings, and just as we went to the bank to get the last check certified, we were notified by the attorney that we had to come up with an additional $10,000. Maurier was able to borrow the money, half from his brother and half from a friend.

People tend to look at us and assume that we are rich, that we have it easy, We aren't, and we don't. We have had the same struggles as other people. We've had to work just as hard for less, but we didn't sit on the sidelines waiting for something to happen. We took the abuse and the rejections, put our hands on the plow, and kept moving forward.

Personal Solvency

Catherine's opinion of me may have been that I was a slug, but my work ethic and efforts did not go unnoticed in the industry. One of the largest banks in the country, the third bank of my career, reached out to me. I like to say they bought me with an offer of $75,000. I gladly accepted.

They were expanding their footprint into the New Jersey market, and they hosted a round of interviews and hired several managers. Among the managers hired were me, Jaxon, and Adam, the son and godson (all of twenty-five years old with no banking experience) of the bank's former Mortgage Manager. At the end of my interview, Sandra Kurzman—interviewer and Market Manager—said, "I will definitely see you again." I knew I had the job.

Jaxon and Adam were placed in established branches in two of the most affluent cities in New Jersey—Princeton and Somerville. I was hired to open a new branch in the low-income city of Elizabeth City, New Jersey—a two and a half hour commute into an unknown community. I didn't recognize the pun intended then, but not only did I look like the people of the community, I also met all the criteria of a protected class—Black, woman, and over the age of forty. I was their token of diversity. My experience was an added bonus for them, and they placed me in the most economically challenged community. I wasn't just valued for my experience and skills. I was also a pawn, a workaround for their government reporting purposes. Again, I just did not understand how to look at the broader picture, how to negotiate from the perspective of my vantage point, to understand my value and what I was bringing to them and not just what they were "giving to me."

Opening the new branch in Elizabeth City gave me an opportunity that challenged me to dig deep and stretch my talents beyond my comfort zone. My job was to build and grow the branch's business by opening accounts, developing and creating partnerships, and gaining the confidence of the community's residents and business owners before actually opening the brick-and-mortar branch. The promise was that if successful, I could expect to be promoted to Area Manager—their version of Regional Manager.

I worked hard, and Maurier worked hard to support me. My life took a hit as well. On Saturdays, so that we could spend time together, Maurier would drive me the two-and-a-half-hour commute to work. While I was in the front office working with customers, he would spend that time in the back break room of the branch studying for his degree.

Given my experience in Harlem, I was successful under the adverse conditions that come with economically challenged communities. Added to that, I had the hostility of the mayor, who vocalized quite often and publicly his disdain for large banks. Before opening the branch, I had exceeded my goal by one hundred and seventy percent and had opened more than a thousand accounts. By the second month, I had expanded my network of partnerships to include the city and county's Economic Development Corporations, Special Improvement District, Chamber of Commerce, Business Improvement District, and the Retail Skills Center. It wasn't easy, and I wasn't always accepted. After being rejected several times by the mayor, I did some research and found out he was interested in Brown Fields *(property developed for industrial purposes that may be complicated by the presence of harmful substances or contamination)*. I used this information as an inducement for him to meet with me for lunch. Before sitting down, he said, "Breaking bread with you will not change my mind. I will never do business with you or any other big bank."

I then created a collaboration between the city's Retail Skills Center and the bank's Recruiting Department and hired more than eighty percent of my staff from the Retail Skills Center. My practice of hiring from the Retail Skills Center increased employment in the city and added a very nice feather to the mayor's cap. When it was time to open my doors, the mayor awarded me a ribbon-cutting ceremony with more press and publicity than I could have ever imagined or done on my own. There is always more than one way to skin a cat.

I was recognized as the highest-performing manager in the area *(area or region refers to a combined number of branches in a geographical area defined by the bank)*, and each time that recognition came with a new and higher goal and/or responsibility. And with each announcement of another success, slick Jaxon would call me to ask how I was doing it. Adam never called; he was just riding Jaxon's coat tail, and I don't think he would have known what to ask.

I found out quite by accident—from a new manager—that my branch was being used at the bank's Training Center all the way in Ohio as the model to follow when opening a new branch. When we introduced ourselves, he said, "Wow, you are Darlene Winston!" *As if I was a celebrity.* "In training, your branch is the model we used for a successful branch opening." Neither my manager nor anyone else at the bank ever shared this —my success story—with me.

A Painful Withdrawal

At the end of that first year, there were three openings for Area Manager. Ronnie, my manager, had been in a meeting all day where they would be notified of the new Area Managers. I was totally confident I would be getting promoted and was anxiously waiting for Ronnie's call to notify me.

As an Area (Regional) Manager, I would manage and impart my skills to the many Branch Managers—usually ten or more—in my assigned area. I knew I could do it. I was already a certified adult trainer, had been a successful Branch Manager in several banks, and a community leader. My success would be exponential.

I was driving through a white-out snowstorm—which added two more hours to my already two-and-a-half-hour commute—when Ronnie called me with the news. Excited. Waiting for her to say it. My heart was beating so fast as I waited for her to tell me I was promoted to Area Manager.

Ronnie said, "I know you worked hard and earned one of these promotions. Unfortunately, you did not get one." My stomach dropped. *I was thirteen again in that room with Nana telling me not to go to the prom after all of the hard work I'd done to earn the right to go.* I could hardly see the snow flying onto the windshield as my tears started to flow. I couldn't speak. I kept swallowing, wanting to gather my thoughts. *Be a big girl; Be a big girl.* I needed to respond professionally. It was still a work environment.

I could not speak. I just listened to her blab on and on. *I couldn't believe that after all of my hard work, I did not get one of the THREE Area Manager positions.* She interrupted my thoughts and said, "Hang in there;

your time is coming, and you will definitely be considered next time." At that very moment, I decided I needed to move on and began to look for other opportunities. If leading the market in sales, being the role model for success in the entire company's Training Center, and creating lasting partnerships for the bank didn't warrant a promotion, nothing would. There was no reason to "hang in there." What more could I possibly do?

Needless to say, two of those positions went to Jaxon and Adam. Jaxon and Adam both showed up at the next meeting driving brand-new matching convertible sports cars. I guess the cars were a package deal, just like the son and godson.

Jaxon was cocky, with his chest puffed out, six feet tall, blond hair acting as if he knew—although not earned—that he would get the promotion, laughing about how he told his wife not to get pregnant anymore because he wanted her to keep her shape. As if we cared or if it had anything to do with his newly-inherited role. Adam, skinny, face pockmarked with acne, stood grinning like a Cheshire cat. As if his every thought came from a bag of rocks. I put on a fake smile, congratulating them and trying to hold it together and still be a team player while the acid in my stomach was churning and bubbling, ready to explode from my mouth.

The next year, my relationship with Sandra Kurzman took a nosedive. My branch had its annual audit. During the audit, the bilingual Teller left her post to translate for a customer and failed to lock her coin safe. The auditor dinged us severely for it. Branch audits are the responsibility of the Operations Manager. Sandra insisted that I take my Operations Manager outside and off of the branch's premises and—as she stated—"Tell her, 'Dammit, this is your fault; get your shit together,' and then fire her." *I was to ream her out and then terminate her?* I refused on all counts, and told Sandra I would not blame her for something that was beyond her control; it was not her fault that we were using a Teller to translate for our customers.

Immediately after this conversation with Sandra, my goals were increased, and I was made to get on daily calls to report my day's activities, the number of sales made, accounts opened, and coaching sessions I had with my Sales team and the results. Basically, I was hazed.

Shortly after the audit, I was contacted for what would be my third unsolicited recruitment for a bank by a headhunter, this time for a Regional

(Area) Manager's position at another bank. I met with Dave Rummage, the new Market Manager for the Northeast market. Dave had been in this new role for about three days. I left the meeting feeling good. My answers were on point, my goals were aligned with the bank's, and I had the experience and knowledge to be successful. Dave said, "I'd like you to meet with the other Regional Managers on the team—they would be your peers and colleagues." The headhunter also called me after my interview and said that Dave was very pleased and to expect an offer. I was excited, finally leaving the bank that had duped me out of a position I'd rightfully earned and then hazed me when I wouldn't fire someone without cause. Good riddance. I looked forward to meeting my future peers.

The meeting was scheduled in Pennsylvania. This was a great short drive—seven minutes from home. I felt good and excited to meet the other team members. I was relaxed. I chose my black skirt suit and white top to wear.

Walking into the conference room, I was not surprised to find I was the only Black person in the room. This is a normal scenario in the banking industry, especially in management, and as I was to learn, more so in this bank. They were a group of three. They sat side by side, unable to recover from their collective shock at my Blackness quickly enough. I chuckled internally at their shock.

After their recovery, introductions were made. Leigh-Ann and Bill were Regional Managers and Tom was their Sales Manager. The three of them sat side by side on one side of the table with a chair in front for me.

Leigh-Ann led the meeting. "Tell us about yourself."

"I have been in retail banking for twenty-nine years. I started as a part-time Teller in New York City and worked my way through the retail side of the bank from Teller to Branch Manager, and Vice President in three large banks. I recently married and now live here in E'Berg," Blah, blah, blah. I wasn't concerned that there weren't any in-depth questions about my responsibilities or goals since this was an introductory meeting and not an interview.

Things were going as expected when Bill jumped in and asked, "Do you have any questions?" I said yes.

As I started to speak, Leigh-Ann interrupted with an announcement to Bill and Tom. "Today is my day to pick up the kiddies." They started a sidebar conversation between the three of them. I sat quietly observing, thinking—*Are they really having a sidebar conversation about their kids?*—and waiting to resume with my answer. When they finished their sidebar, Bill turned to me and said, "Thank you for coming in; it was nice meeting you." And that was it—an abrupt, awkward end to what was supposed to be a meeting of acquaintances. I was struck with confusion. *Did I miss the memo? Because this was anything but friendly. Was I on a bad date? Was their cue to end the meeting an announcement to pick up the kids?* They continued to talk among themselves as if I were intruding on their conversation.

Needless to say, I did not get the offer. The position went to Richard Dover—all of a five-foot-tall Napoleon Bonaparte look-alike. Richard was personal friends with Bill, Leigh-Ann, and Tom. They had grown up together in the bank and in the same neighborhood. Their families ate dinner together on Sundays and vacationed together in the summers. They raised their children together, and their children attended school together. "My future peers and colleagues" never intended to give any positive feedback about me from this meeting. They were merely completing a task and appeasing Dave, their new manager.

9
A New Account

Deeper into the Bearish Market

The aggressive sales tactics and goals were more than many could muster, and by this time most of the Branch Managers who were hired to increase the bank's New Jersey footprint had left and gone on to other banks. They were leaving in droves.

Later that year, my friend and former colleague told me that her bank (the same one that had recruited me for the Regional Manager's position) was looking for a Branch Manager in one of their New Jersey branches. The branch was fifty miles closer to home. I applied and was hired.

When I announced my resignation, the Human Resources Manager, Carrie Tucker, called me. She asked, "Why would you leave now? We've thrown everything at you, *to make you fail*, and you succeeded," as if I had passed some test. Wow, they had really devised a plan to set me up to fail. I know I have taken some crap from my White female managers while trying to succeed in my career, but why would I continue to work for a company that verbalized and boldly admitted they had set me up for failure? Even I had higher standards than to stay there.

I simply replied, "I manage my own career."

Despite its ending, two of the accomplishments I am most proud of during my time in New Jersey were encouraging the bank to support the New Jersey State Firemen's Mutual Benevolent Association (NJFMBA) to support the Fallen Heroes of 9/11, and representing the bank as the team leader for the Habitat for Humanity Initiative in Elizabeth City.

My new employer's sales goals were no different from the old one, and many managers cited various cultural differences and left this bank for other opportunities, as well. After two years of solid success under my belt, a Regional Manager's position became available, and I applied. My interview was scheduled with Dave, who also now had two years under his belt as Market Manager.

Dave called to say that my in-person interview was canceled and a telephone interview would be scheduled instead. During the telephone interview, totally from out in left field, Dave opened with, "When are you leaving?"

Huh? Leaving?

"All of your peers from your former bank have left, so when are you leaving?"

I answered, "Dave, I have nothing to do with anyone else's actions. I have to manage my own career." There were no further questions, and the "interview" was over. He opened the interview only to close it. If he really thought I was leaving, why would I apply for another position? Perhaps he wanted me to go, but I never considered myself a threat, and I was certainly not a follower.

The following week, we had an off-site meeting, and Dave introduced us to our new Regional Manager. It was clear I was never a consideration. He had already hired someone else when we had my "telephone interview."

Our new manager opened with, "I don't know why Dave hired me. I don't know anything about this job."

Dave said, "Don't worry; we will make you successful."

Wow. What a slap in the face. She *openly* and unashamedly admitted that she knew nothing about the job but was given a nice pat on the back and public support for her acceptance and ignorance. I worked hard to suppress the mixed emotions of disgust and rejection that seemed to keep triumphing over me in the hands of poor leadership and unqualified hires. The cycle seemed never-ending, but it only added fuel to my fire. I knew I could work harder, and keep at it, and I would get to my goal—eventually.

The following year, the bank developed a new job family called the Private Customer Group. I was forced to accept that I would never become a Regional Manager while Dave was the Market Manager. The Private

Customer Group was a timely opportunity for me to shift gears and move my career in a different direction. The bank's vision of the Private Customer Group was to create an elite book of business for clients with large balances. The requirements of the Private Customer Group's Team Leader were to have investment licenses and manage a staff who would only work with customers with larger portfolios and investable assets.

Having all of my investment licenses, and having managed investment-licensed employees who managed large client portfolios in three other large banks including this one, I met the criteria. I was a perfect fit. How much easier could it be? An internal candidate who knows the company, knows the clients, and has led successful investment teams. *Yep, a shoo-in.* This is it. An opportunity for me to switch gears.

I applied for the Private Customer Group Team Leader position and was interviewed by the hiring manager. Within the hour, on my drive home, the recruiter called me to say, "The hiring manager really liked you and asked if you would return the following morning to meet her manager, Stephen Lewis."

As I walked into Stephen's office the next morning, he looked at me as if I had two heads. *Ah, they didn't share with him that I was a Black woman. I won't be getting this job.* Looking around his office, I guessed his wife must have decorated it. It had bistro-style, wrought iron chairs with checkered-top metal tables you would see in a garden. At six feet, two inches, and with a bad back, I could barely fit in the chair. I had to hold on to support my back, and the chair almost tipped over.

Stephen looked at me with cold indifference, disdain, and a smirk on his face, as if it tickled him that I almost fell off of the chair. He asked very few questions but none about the position. Probably about the weather. Who knows? I checked out after the first off-topic question. I had been here before, and I already knew the outcome of this checkbox behavior to respect corporate policy. This was the dog-and-pony show, and I was not interested in playing the game today. I disassociated completely, and I think that helped us both move toward the decision we both knew was coming. I was not hired. I took my energy elsewhere. I constantly scoured the job openings for opportunities. I was certain there had to be a position for me. Later that year, another Private Customer Group Team Leader position became available. I applied.

Ironically, one of the people on the interview panel was the person whom Stephen hired for the first Team Leader position I applied for. During the interview, he blurted out, "Hands down you qualify. Look at all your credentials; they hired me, and I didn't even know half the things you know. My good buddy Stephen called me and said he had a job for me and that they'd train me." No wonder Stephen had nothing to say in my interview. He had already given the job to his "good buddy."

The wind of confidence I had deflated like a popped balloon. How could he have sat there silently and fully aware that the job was already promised to someone else? That comment left me to balance skepticism and optimism. After all, it was a compliment, but what did his statement mean for this go-round? *Well, we will see what happens this time.*

When I left the interview room, I noticed Jeffrey, my branch's Investment Banker, sitting in the lobby. When he saw me, he blanched and looked mortified as if he was going to piss his pants because he had called out of work that day stating his wife was ill.

When he recovered from his shock, he told me he may as well leave, that he doesn't have a chance at this job when compared to my experience. *You think? This job is two levels above yours, and you are failing as an employee and are on warning for failure to do your job of having investment conversations with customers. How are you going to lead a team of investment bankers?* I told him good luck and left.

Interestingly, Stephen not only hired Jeffrey, but he also became Jeffrey's mentor. Years later, I saw Jeffrey at a meeting, and he said, "I still don't know how I got that job over you; I guess Stephen really likes me because he has put me up for two other promotions since then." But I knew. My experience had already taught me that White men and women didn't need experience to be promoted or hired into a position at this bank. I was never going to be a White man or woman, but my experience must count for something. *Right?* Surely my experience and successes were worth overlooking my Blackness to move me up within the company.

Obviously, I had not shined enough. I stopped looking for opportunities and spent the next two years plugging away, succeeding at my goals and winning small accolades and paper awards for my successes. I was convinced my experience coupled with continued successes would make me an undeniable, solid *yes* for my next role. That's what I was after.

10
Payment Failed

Defeated, I applied for the Branch Manager position in the E'Berg branch. If I had no opportunity for growth, then I may as well be close to home. It was a seven-minute drive from my house. Unlike the branch I was leaving, with its high balances, elite customers, and airline pilots who lived on the lake, E'Berg was *the* failing branch in Dave's market. The E'Berg branch was in the region where the headhunter sought me for Regional Manager years earlier. I was quite familiar with the branch because it was where I'd met Leigh-Ann, Bill, and Tom for that acquaintance meeting. And guess who would be my manager? Richard Dover—yep, the very same Napoleon Bonaparte look-alike. The irony. No one wanted to manage E'Berg. It was failing by all counts. At the interview, Richard's final words to me were, "Your priority and my expectation is that you eliminate the entire team and rebuild the branch."

Once I was offered the position I started receiving emails from every employee in the E'Berg branch. TJ, the Banker, said, "I was told when I was hired that I could leave early every day because I am a single father and have to be home when my children get there." I just chuckled. Yeah, fat chance buddy; show it to me in writing.

Evelyn, the Customer Service Representative, said, "They said you were going to fire all of us. Do you know when that will happen? I have three kids and need to look for another job." On and on they went with constant concerns about me, the big bad wolf, coming to fire the entire staff. I wonder what idiot (Richard Dover) told them that? Is this really the message he gave them when he hired me? *Jeez.*

This team was so broken from the constant barrage of abuse they received from Richard and senior management. It was really bad there. I had my work cut out for me. I love a good challenge, but dang. Well, at least I lived down the street; no more driving hours from work through white-out snow storms.

First things first. I scheduled a meeting with the entire team. I told them I was not there to terminate anyone unless there was cause. So let's get that out of our heads. Second, my goal was for us to work together to fix those things that have come apart in the branch and to change the perception that management has about us.

We talked in general about the concerns senior management had with our branch and how we would correct them. I told them about my background and asked them to each share with the group how long they'd been at the bank, what their job was now, and what were some things they'd like to see changed in the branch.

I shared that my plan of action was to get us moving in a direction that would get us positive recognition. We would meet weekly as a team to discuss the branch's goals and how we would get back on track. We would have a daily meeting at eight o'clock each morning, except Saturday, to discuss the objective for the day. And finally, I would have a weekly one-on-one with each employee to discuss their individual goals and concerns. Together we would build a branch that included their individual plans for success. I gained their trust and their buy-in and assured them we could and would be a top-performing branch and rebuild respect for our branch.

My first meeting was with TJ. I wanted to address his email to me and discuss how we would proceed together. I told him I couldn't find a policy in the bank where we hired anyone with a condition that they leave early. TJ said, "Yes, that is what they told me when I was hired. I have it in writing."

I said, "Great; send me a copy of that agreement so I can make sure that we include it in our future plans. In the meantime, let's discuss your needs and how we can support you, and then we will discuss your personal goals and how they align with the future of our branch." I never received the written agreement, and it was not brought up again.

My next meeting was with Evelyn. I first apologized that she was given the message that I was hired to terminate everyone in the branch and told her I found nothing in her records to indicate she was in jeopardy of losing her job. I reiterated I had no reason to terminate anyone without cause. I wanted to talk about her career and expectations and how I could support them, along with my expectations of her and for the future of the branch.

I assured everyone that we all had an equal say in how we would proceed to be the best branch in the market. With no further threat of losing their jobs looming over their heads, the team settled down. We got down to business. I got to know their families, and they knew mine. We shared celebrations, we shared failures, and at our daily meetings, we committed to each other to be our best.

One step at a time, we removed all the barriers we controlled to have individual and team successes. I believed the challenge to turn this branch around would also demonstrate to Dave Rummage that my successes and credentials were earned, prove myself, and assure him I was qualified to lead a region.

Our first objective was to clean up the branch's errors and recover from the past two years of failed audits. We passed the next two audits with ninety-five and ninety, respectively. We were so proud and ecstatic, but acknowledged we had gotten sloppy with the second audit where we dropped from ninety-five percent to ninety percent.

The next goal was to rebuild relationships with our clients. We scheduled appointments, hosted after-hours customer appreciation events, and began mending fences. Using the same tactics I'd used when hearing the employee's concerns to hear the client's concerns with the bank, we started repairing those broken relationships.

In the interim, the bank had started using the Gallup Poll to measure employee and customer success and engagement. This was a great way for us to also measure our successes without reinventing the wheel. We gradually started receiving positive recognition for our successes in sales. We increased our branch's overall service performance, ranked number one in our peer group of fifty-three branches for overall sales revenue growth, and we increased employee and customer engagement.

We received the Gallup Poll Human Sigma Six Honorable Mention, and then in succession, we won the Human Sigma Six award the next four quarters. This honor was only awarded to the top ten percent of employees in the company. Now consistently the best of the best, we were extremely proud. Surely with this huge turnaround and company recognition from their newest Gallup Polled measure for success, I had definitely proven myself to be a candidate for the next Regional Manager's position.

The team proudly displayed our awards on their desks and around the branch. They were constant reminders that we were not who they tried to label us to be. We were a winning team. I was never better than my team, never their boss, but always their leader. We worked tirelessly side by side every day.

I'm proud to say I did not terminate one employee from this team. As a result of our success, employee development was imminent. I had the opportunity to promote the Assistant Branch Manager to become a Merchant Services Account Executive; Evelyn, our Customer Service Representative to be my Assistant Branch Manager; a Teller to become a Teller Supervisor; and TJ became a top-performing Investment Banker in the region. I also promoted my Teller Supervisor to become a Branch Manager (she recently became a Regional Manager). She said I was the first call she made when promoted to say thank you for believing in her and creating a path to leadership. My heart burst with pride. *This is why I do what I do. I love helping people who would not have otherwise been given an opportunity.*

As they were promoted and positions opened up, we started getting calls from other employees around the company asking how they could be a part of our branch team. We were very selective, and when these requests arose, the entire team researched to find out who the person was, why they wanted to join our team, and if they would be a good fit.

Hands down, this was the best team I've ever managed in my career. Together we had arguably one of the most successful branches in Dave's market. With respect, empathy, and human kindness, I was able to uncover and tap into talent no one believed we had and achieved accomplishments no one ever dreamed possible. We were recognized company-wide for our successes.

I have a reputation in both my personal and professional life for holding people to high standards, with a hard line around accountability but always with kindness, fairness, and respect. I believe the best managers lead by example, respect their employees as people, and hold them accountable for the job they've taught them to do. It's my motto, and I am very proud to stand by this in every situation.

The bank was also acquiring more banks and had to expand its Human Resources Department to meet industry standards for a "large bank." Given my continued success and demonstration of leadership, Richard

Dover asked me to train my peers on how to formulate a business plan, and he also nominated me to participate in the new Diversity Equity and Inclusion (DEI) Project for the market. DEI was later canceled. It appeared that once we started getting deep into the company's racial disparities, the project was disbanded. Admittedly, I was right up front and center and asked about the hiring practices and lack of diversity at the top of the company. I also shared my past interview experiences—or lack thereof—with the group.

Even now, I find that Diversity, Equity, and Inclusion is a buzz term presented to the public as if the organization wants change. However, in my experience, I've found that in many cases the organizations claiming to want Diversity, Equity, and Inclusion rarely put their words into action.

Timing is Everything

Richard Dover was terminated. It was rumored for failure to do his job. *No! Really? How could he be fired for failure to do his job with so many friends? Hmmm?* The rumor was spreading like wildfire throughout the market. We'd never heard of a Regional Manager being fired.

Timing is everything. I had come full circle and had proven myself to be a strong manager and leader. It was time for me to move on and pursue my dream of becoming a Regional Manager. I applied once again for the now-open Regional Manager position—Richard's position. With all the accolades to accompany the experience I demonstrated, I believed this was my time. The turnaround of the E'Berg Branch under my leadership and my successes should solidly land me in a position for growth and opportunity in the market and company. I should definitely be the top contender. I knew the region, I knew the market, I knew the players, I was a leader among my peers, I was a proven success, and a member of the community.

I applied for the position and was scheduled to meet with Dave for an interview. He canceled, yet again. I assumed he would reschedule. However, walking into our monthly meeting, as if seeing me triggered a reminder he had canceled my interview, Dave stopped me right outside of the conference room door and told me I was not being chosen for the position. I was unable to concentrate, defeated, and rejected yet again, but had to *"be a Big Girl"* and put on my team player face.

In that meeting, Dave announced that he was creating a Super Region—the first in the company—by consolidating two regions—ours with the Western region—to be run by that Regional Manager, Donna.

When we met Donna, she shared with us how she got her job as a Regional Manager. She said that when she was a Banker, her manager had health problems and resigned. After some months when restructuring the region, all the employees' names were put in an envelope with their new positions on it. When her name was pulled, it said *Regional Manager*. She said that she recognized the mistake and immediately notified the Market Manager and showed him the paper with her name on it. He assured her there was no mistake, and she got the "we'll make you successful" tap on the shoulder. This is the person who would now manage the only Super Region—twenty-six branches—in the company.

As we worked together, and I shared my experiences, Donna and I became friendly. Donna also told me that Dave was giving her a tough time. In their one-on-one meeting, she asked him if he had the choice, would he have hired her to be a Regional Manager? He told her, "No."

It never occurred to me to leave the company. Seven years in, I had invested too much, and I kept believing my hard work would get me my just due. However, my lack of "connections" and my skin color squarely placed me out of the running every time. Additionally, Maurier was still growing his business and trying to gain name recognition in his industry while also studying to become a minister at church and finishing his master's degree. He would spend days on the phone trying to secure contracts, and sometimes they didn't come for months. At one point, he even went back to a corporate job to make ends meet. Mine was the only guaranteed income for a long period of time. In addition to my conditioned beliefs that I didn't deserve boundaries, I was going to eat as much crow at work as I had to. I was not going to blow up our lives because someone hurt my feelings.

In the interim, there was a lot of movement in the market. Dave promoted Leigh-Ann to Market Manager, now leaving that Regional Manager's position open. By now I knew her as the sixty-year-old dancer/ event entertainer of the company. Dave had always seemed to have a certain affinity for her. All the men in the market did. I think they enjoyed the fact that she was the entertainment at every event. She was like the failed cheerleader of the market. All the White men would gather around with beers in hand, jeering, and ask her if she'd be dancing at the event. Leigh-

Ann would giddily—like a five-year-old—say yes and that she needed to change. She'd then scurry off and put on her "tutu," and then she'd dance around the place, her curly blond hair bobbing around her head, tap dancing and gyrating her skinny hips. It was quite embarrassing to see a grown woman doing these antics at work. I reflected on the lesson that Jane tried to teach me so long ago. People will do anything for power.

I applied for the open Regional Manager's position. As I started doing my research and preparing for the interview, I was surprised, actually shocked, to find that Leigh-Ann's region only had a sixty-eight percent success rate. I was shocked that she could have been promoted to a Market Manager's position when she had a failed region. She must have gotten the "we'll make you successful" tap on the shoulder because instead of getting fired for her failed region, she was now in charge of eight regions. It appeared that she gyrated herself right into a promotion.

The third time's a charm, right? Surely this was my time. I had turned the failing branch in the market around to be the most successful. I coached Branch Managers on how to be successful and build business plans, and I was on the Market Diversity Initiative. I hit on all cylinders. I thought.

Dave scheduled an interview with me. This time I decided to be proactive and allow him to come clean. I asked what was he looking for in a candidate. He said he was looking for someone who lived and worked in that area. I lived about thirty minutes away. That was close enough, considering the distance between the branches and all the commuting I'd already demonstrated I was willing to do. I didn't think that would be the determining criteria to eliminate me from getting this position.

Dave hired Seth—White of course. When Dave introduced Seth, he said Seth was born in the area hospital, however, his family immediately moved and he was raised, lived, and worked in California. Ironically, so did Robert Thompson, the Territory Manager and Dave's boss. It looks like the "live and work" in the area criteria did not apply to Seth, *since California was 2700 miles away and just a mere forty-one-hour commute.*

With all the bank's acquisitions and mergers, it was now considered a large bank, and it had to show on record how it was including people of the protected class in its hiring practices. Once again I fit all of the criteria of a protected class—Black, female, over the age of forty—and every time I applied for a position and Dave scheduled an interview with me, he was able to say that he interviewed a diverse group of candidates. I was being made a mockery of.

I applied for these positions naively believing that my hard work and successes would get me the promotion. I thought it before but was forced to accept it now. I would never have an opportunity to grow in Dave Rummage's market. I continued to maintain my success as a Branch Manager but began seeking other opportunities outside of Dave's scope.

After the "work in the same area and Super Region incidents," I applied for an open Regional Manager's position back in New Jersey. *Why not?* I had nothing left to lose. When Dave scheduled the interview, and having been down this road three other times with Dave, I asked him if he would give me detailed feedback if I was not the selected candidate. He said he didn't believe in moving a Branch Manager into a Regional Manager's position. So even before the interview, he had already decided I would not be the candidate, *but he would use my interview to meet the protected class quota.*

He hired a Branch Manager—A white male, the cousin of another Regional Manager. I was playing nice in the sandbox, but my sandbox was in a different park.

This pattern of Dave telling me what he wasn't looking for was a guise to reveal what he was going to do and who he was actually going to hire. I saw this pattern again and again. It was the slap in the face that I had gotten used to. It didn't stop me from showing up to seek the next opportunity, but it certainly drained my enthusiasm.

I checked the internal job posting site daily and applied for every Regional Manager's position that became available in every state in the company. I was frantic. My vulnerabilities were recognizable, I was circling the drain, and my need to be rewarded for my successes was palatable. This desperation made me an easy target and set me up to be used as a check box, the example of the diverse pool, "the protected class" of candidates interviewed for said position. However, the end result was always the same. Promotions went to White men and women who rarely made their goals but instead hung around water coolers and golf courses, whose parents went to school together, or whose friend at work had a friend. As the cliché goes, it's not about what you know. It's about who you know. The connections you have.

Maurier, always supportive, drove me up and down the Eastern Seaboard for interviews. I applied in Baltimore, twice in Washington, DC, and every other state that had an opening for a Regional Manager. I was beginning to feel like Dave Rummage was notifying every Market Manager that I was coming. I would leave the interviews excited and hopeful, only to have my feelings dashed by the time I returned home. The feedback after each interview was always the same. "We love you. Your interview was the best. You'll hear from us in a couple of days. You made it really hard for us to decide."

One hiring manager called me himself—instead of relaying the message through Human Resources—and said, "I wanted to reach out to you myself. You are a great candidate for the role. Your interview and credentials made it a difficult choice for me. However, before interviewing you, I had already selected another candidate from my team"—my experience made me presume that it was *a White male*.

I just sat there in my office, tears forming—not falling but blurring my sight. I couldn't show my emotions with my customers and staff milling about. I just had to suck it up and move on. Embarrassed and disappointed yet again, I had to go home and tell Maurier that once again I did not get the position. He would have to be wondering why I would come out of these interviews with such hope and excitement but yet was never chosen.

In this instance, I think my application must have gotten in before the job requisition was removed from the site since the policy at the bank was that if a qualified internal candidate's application was received before the open position was removed from the job search site, the hiring manager must interview the candidate. This practice was especially deceptive and misleading for the internal candidates, and it gave us false hope.

11
Major Market Move

To increase its footprint and grow in size, our bank was acquiring lots of banks. We were gobbling them up like Pac-Man. *It was also about the time that Maurier and I purchased some land in the South, thinking ahead about our future retirement home.* So a year later, when the announcement was made that we were acquiring a bank in the South, I immediately raised my hand to be a part of the conversion team. The conversion team was responsible for training the employees of the acquired bank and getting them acclimated to our systems. I believed that this would give me some exposure, leverage, and an opportunity to prove myself in a new market away from Dave Rummage.

In addition to being a part of the conversion team, I also applied for two other positions in the new market. I applied for the Sales Manager position, and I was contacted by the recruiter for the Bank at Work Department and asked if I would consider being the Market Manager for the Bank at Work Program in the new market. Though she never said it, I believe that Donna recommended me for this opportunity. She was as excited as I was. Without hesitation, I said yes.

I met with and interviewed with the hiring manager for the Bank at Work position. At the end of the interview, he said, "As a formality, I'd like to schedule a meeting for you to meet my manager. I will notify you tomorrow."

After several days and no communication, I reached out to him, but he didn't return any of my calls or emails. We were in a meeting when I finally received a call from the recruiter. I was excited, thinking this was the offer call. She apologized. She said she was given the green light to move forward with me; however, things changed. The hiring manager I'd met with was not aware that his boss was saving the position for someone else and that he was also being displaced.

My head was about to burst; the pressure exploding on the inside could've set off an atomic bomb. *Saving? What? How was this even legal?!!!!! How does this keep happening?!!!! Does anybody else see this?*

After leaving the meeting, all I could do was sit there in my car holding tightly onto the steering wheel with tears streaming down my face. There were too many tears to see clearly to drive. Just like my career, I was stuck. I couldn't see a way forward. I was only left with tears and no resolve.

I let the tears run their course in the parking lot of yet another meeting two hours away from home. I forced myself to get it together as I prepared for the long drive. I later discovered that Paul, with the bright red hair, was from the acquired bank and the great benefactor of the "saved" position.

Once Paul was on board, I was asked—or voluntold—to help him prepare a presentation and model of the Bank at Work Program for the market because he didn't understand or know the program. I gave him some brief pointers, but he still did not grasp the concept. He was an Investment Banker by trade and clueless about retail banking. How do you teach someone who has never managed anything how to manage an entire market when they haven't even had any basic leadership experience? *I want to be a doctor, but it wouldn't make me one just because I show up at a hospital.*

A few weeks later, I got wind that they had started interviewing for the Sales Manager position, however, no one had reached out to me. (The Sales Manager is responsible for coaching the Sales staff in the branch while the Regional Manager coaches the Branch Managers.) I called Charles, the Regional Manager handling the hiring of the position. Charles scheduled me, and I was interviewed by Charles, Ray, also a Regional Manager, and Tammy. I'm not sure to this day what Tammy's role was. They were all from the acquired bank. I wondered what they would ask me since they were all from the incoming bank and admittedly didn't know what a Sales Manager was or did.

I quickly learned that instead of being interviewed for the position, I was instead there to give them a tutorial on the position. The interview was just a barrage of questions; I felt like I was on a firing squad. What do they do? What should we expect? How do we do it? Can you describe what it would look like? Brad, a Branch Manager from Chicago, taller than average with an auburn-colored quiff haircut, was given the job. I'm sure Brad's wealthy mother-in-law, with a household name in town who knew Charles the hiring manager, helped.

Whether at a meeting with his superiors, or peers, or when visiting the branches, Brad was loud, obnoxious, and boisterous, and known for telling off-color jokes and making inappropriate comments. It was rumored that his inappropriate comments were what had his head on the chopping block in Chicago and that this relocation was his last stop. He was known as the jokester. No one ever took him seriously and certainly not the Branch Managers he was responsible for coaching.

After these two incidents and everything that followed, I quickly realized that while we were the acquiring bank, the acquired bank was in charge. Unlike in prior acquisitions, we were not allowed on the premises or to train any of their employees until the day we took over. They literally closed their doors on Friday evening, and we opened on Monday morning with our name and signage. That entire weekend was spent changing over computers, systems, and signage.

When their employees returned on Monday morning, they had never seen or touched any of our computers or systems. This is what we, the conversion team, were responsible for. Our directive was to stand behind each employee and verbally tell them which buttons to push, but we were not allowed to touch any of the computers ourselves. It was chaotic and asinine. A pure shit show, if you ask me, and an awful experience for all involved. I don't know how desperate we were to get into the South, but it was clear that the acquired bank was also allowed to take all the prime positions for its employees while we were left to train them.

There were lines were out the doors of every branch across the South with customers coming in to withdraw all their money and close accounts, and they would only speak to the employees they were familiar with—those from the acquired bank. It was like a fire sale.

One customer, when asked why she was closing her account, said, "I hate the color orange, and your debit cards are orange." Of course, we had personalized cards, but she refused.

While I was training the employees, the Branch Manager, Mark– mid-twenties, six feet three inches tall, looking like a young Steve McQueen, well-groomed for the golf course—said, "Don't waste your time training me because I'm going to be a Business Banker."

I replied, "Does your staff know?" And he said no, the position isn't posted yet.

I asked how he knew, and he winked at me and said, "It's already done."

Mark was no loss to the branch team. They constantly complained that when he wasn't out playing golf, all he did was sit in his office with his shoes off and his feet up on his desk.

At the end of the conversion, I took the branch staff out to dinner. As we sat around talking, I shared with them that I was planning a family reunion. Janice, the Banker, asked if my family would be eating fried chicken and watermelon and wearing big hats at my family reunion while the rest of them openly snickered. I was deeply disturbed and annoyed by their ignorance. I said I hadn't decided on the menu yet and asked her if that's what her family ate at their reunions. All of a sudden, a hush came over the table. I gave myself a mental high-five and a "Touché, Darlene."

After the conversion, I returned home to Pennsylvania and back to my branch. Two months later, just as he said, Mark was promoted to Business Banker. Charles reached out to me and asked if I would consider coming back down south to manage the branch I had converted—Mark's branch.

By this time, I'd invested so many years into this bank and had applied for a vast number of positions and opportunities in the Northeast and saw all those positions go to people who were not persons of color. Again, what did I have to lose? Additionally, I knew the team from conversion.

I decided to try the new Southern market. I believed it might be my last opportunity to grow within the bank. I told each member of my E'berg team, individually and then as a team, of my decision to relocate. Recognizing that this was the end of an era for us, we were emotional.

Maurier was concerned about us having a long-distance marriage and the impact this move would have on our family. I believed our marriage was solid and could withstand anything if we worked together. I also reminded Maurier that we already had a long-distance marriage since he spent the weekdays in New York for his business and came home on weekends. Also, I rationalized to him that it took less time for him to fly down South than it did for him to drive from New York to Pennsylvania.

Maurier reluctantly agreed, having lived with the stress of me trying to find other positions.

During that first year, to try and maintain some stability in my family life, Maurier and I opened the Pennsylvania house to continue the tradition of hosting Thanksgiving dinner. I flew up on Tuesday so we could shop and get the house ready for overnight guests and others. We'd then clean up and close the house back up, and I flew back on Monday to meet my grind, and Maurier went back to New York to manage his business.

The cost of moving South was very steep, emotionally and financially. It created a wedge in my marriage that I didn't expect, and Charles would only give me the position if I took a ten-thousand-dollar pay cut with a five-thousand-dollar relocation stipend. This move was a significant hardship, but I believed I had no other options. I was determined to grow my career, *and they owed me*. I had proven myself in more ways than one. I desperately needed to get away from the toxicity of discrimination, and racism that violated me in the Northeast market. At this point, I would have done anything, and I sacrificed everything.

The South

By the time all the logistics were ironed out, and I was finally physically moved, Mark had moved on into his Business Banker role, and the team had started viewing Janice, the Banker, as their leader. The branch staff would ignore me and go to Janice for directions and then they would be frustrated when I reversed her decisions. It was an uphill battle. Mark, now a Business Banker, would also schedule appointments for Janice to accompany him on business calls, and when I would say no, he looked incredulous. One day, he finally asked me why. I told him Janice was not the manager; he could schedule anything for her or with her, but until he had a conversation with me first, the answer would always be no. It never happened again, and the branch team started following the chain of command as well.

I don't think they had ever seen a Black person as a Branch Manager in this part of the South. A few Black customers came in and said they couldn't believe it, that this was a first, and they would ask if I was really the manager.

This move South was only a lateral move, and I quickly demonstrated my value. I led the branch to become the number-one performing branch in our region. Employee and customer engagement also increased, and we were quickly recognized. By the end of my fourth month, our production results had doubled in some areas and tripled in others, and we were leading the region in lending and new account sales. I also became a certified advocate for women in business and was asked to represent the market at the Teller Supervisor Forum to share best practices and tools for success.

Meanwhile, all the clichés were in play in this move. Moving from the frying pan into the fire was an understatement. The grass isn't always greener . . . You never miss the water . . . I was lonely in the South. The people there were probably the most unfriendly I had ever encountered. My all-White staff would publicly plan after-work activities, and although aware I was living down there alone, I was never invited to participate. They were awful, unkind, and cruel.

I would walk into the branch, and an immediate hush would come over the office. It was palpable. When I would walk out of the office, I could almost feel and hear the building vibrate when it came alive as they resumed what I could surmise were conversations about me. I had four strikes against me. I represented the new bank, I was their manager, I was Black, and I was from the North—a Yankee, as they call us—or Yankee N— —r, as I imagined they called me. They did not want me or the bank with all of its sales goals, high accountability, and expectations.

Their cruelty was openly hostile. One day I heard Irene, a part-time Teller–gray-haired or faded blonde—telling the rest of the staff that there was a bridge being closed. Naturally concerned since I lived across the bridge, I asked which bridge was closing. No one answered. So I said, calling her name, "Irene, which bridge is it?" She would not answer me. I could not believe it. Who does this? Refuse to speak when asked a direct question. Unfortunately, this was just one example of the level of meanness there. I just stayed my course.

Irene liked reading, and I'd noticed that she was fond of one particular author. When she retired, I bought her the newest release of that author's book. As she was expressing her appreciation to me, her sidekick Peggy interrupted and said, "Irene, "don't believe that shit. That's not a sincere gift." I ignored Peggy's comment and kept walking. I took it for what it was worth. Peggy was probably unhappy about her own life and could not imagine a nice gesture. She was not yet thirty with six kids and still living with her "Mama and Stepdaddy," as she often referred to them.

Of all the transitions, this was like nothing I'd ever known. I was miserable, and it didn't help that I had no family with me. I was lonely. I reflected on these feelings one morning in the parking lot as I waited to start my day. I called Maurier choked with emotion and tears, and said, "I don't think I can do this.

He said "Yes you can. You've done it before." Dismissing my concerns, he moved on to talk about something else.

I don't know if I was encouraged or felt more lonely and isolated since it mirrored the standard answer I'd gotten all of my life whenever I shared my fears or concerns. Either way, it confirmed my belief of why bother and to continue to keep my feelings to myself.

The insults and unanticipated comments continued from the staff for the next year and a half. It was the craziest and most unexpected of things. For instance, one day I told Janice, the Banker, that her dress was nice, and she replied, "It's hard to keep up when Michelle Obama has such great arms." I thought, *WHAT!? Did I miss something?*

In addition to getting prime positions, the employees of the acquired bank were also allowed to keep their above-range salaries for an additional year. The agreement was that each employee used that year to find a job to match their salary. Any employee who had not found a new position would receive a ten percent salary decrease to be within our salary ranges. However, to avoid cutting the salaries of those employees, the Regional and Market Managers created Assistant Manager positions—no experience necessary—within the branches to promote those employees. Janice was one of those employees. Janice was also constantly telling me that she and Charles, my manager, were neighbors and friends. I guess this was her not-so-subliminal threat to me.

So it was no surprise when Janice came to me and stated—as if this was a done deal—that she wanted to be the Assistant Manager in our branch. I told her we didn't need an Assistant Manager to manage one Banker and three part-time Tellers, and if we did, she was not ready to be an Assistant Manager. However, I would be willing to coach and train her so she would be in the best position if the opportunity became available. She said okay. I gave her some small leadership responsibilities to start with. After a week, she said she was not interested.

However, a few days later, she asked if she could leave early to go to her daughter's school. I said, of course. Shortly after Janice left, Charles called me to say Janice had come to his office to discuss being an Assistant Manager in the branch, and he wanted me to reconsider her for the position. I was livid. She lied, and he took a meeting with one of my employees without informing me. I was so angry. I asked if he was in his office. He said yes. I told him I wanted to meet with him and I was on my way. I hung up the phone. I don't think that I gave him a chance to answer. I needed to have a face-to-face with him. He needed to understand the seriousness of this and also how critical this was to my managing effectively.

When I arrived, I still hadn't cooled down. I stormed into his office and sat down at his desk, not giving him a chance to speak. I said, "Charles, you hired me to manage my branch, and as we discussed before, I do not need an Assistant Manager. I need to know if you will continue to entertain my employees' complaints, allowing them to go over my head whenever they're not happy."

Taken aback and surprised at my honesty and brazenness, he emphatically said, "You have nothing to worry about. Furthermore, Janice lives in my community, and we are not friends." He kept his word.

I reflected on the Assistant Manager situation; the Michelle Obama comment; and the fried chicken, watermelon, and big hat comments at the conversion dinner. These racially-charged incidents with Janice were escalating. I knew I had to get ahead of this and get it on record, so I notified Human Resources. I did not want any potential future retaliatory complaints or accusations from Janice. Cathy, the Human Resources Representative, told me "You have to understand that Janice is a White woman of a certain age from the South and that she doesn't mean you any harm. I'll speak to her." *With her Southern twang, it sounded more like, "Ya have to understain' that Jane-iss is a Waat woman of a certain edge from the South and that she dod'nt mean ya any harm."*

As I had come to do about so many of the decisions made in this bank, I wondered, *WHAT? Who ever heard of such a thing?* Cathy circled back with me and said Janice assured her she didn't mean anything by it and asked if I wanted to pursue it further. I said no; I merely wanted it on record should we have any further unexpected incidents. Once again, an apology is supposed to assuage the purposeful pain inflicted on a person of color by the harmful actions of the privileged, and we are expected to just accept it and move on. *Unbelievable!*

It became clear in more ways than one that Cathy had apparently spoken with Janice. I imagined it was probably more like, "Them Yankee N— —s don't understand how we roll down here." (Probably sounding like dem Yankee N— —s dod'nt understain' how we roll down here). Two days later I was sitting in my office and looked up from my computer. I was startled that someone was there. There stood Janice's husband, all of six feet and five inches, standing threateningly and blocking the entire width and height of my office doorway, glaring at me, never saying a word, with just an angry and threatening scowl on his face. *This motherfucker must really want some trouble. I hope I don't have to have Maurier come down here and fuck him up.* Never blinking, just staring right back at him, he turned and walked away, as if he was confident I got the message. I hoped he had gotten mine as well.

After three months in his role as Sales Manager, Brad finally visited my branch. He asked if I could help him put together his Employee Engagement presentation for the Branch Managers—since I had been a repeat reward recipient. He then said, "Just so you know, the reason I don't visit your branch is because you know the job. Perhaps better than I do." *You'd think, since rumor has it you were on the cusp of being fired in Chicago when your mama-in-law and Charles pulled your ass out of the fire.* Sitting on my credenza with a smug and stupid grin on his face, he said, "However, when I get my next promotion to Regional Manager, you can have my job."

I said, "No thanks; I'll be your competition." He knew he had not beaten me out of the Sales Manager position because of his skills but because of his connections.

I continued to pursue my dream of becoming a Regional Manager. In general, the employees from the incoming bank were not doing well under our hard sales structure. They were fleeing to other local banks that shared their soft sales culture.

I'd proven myself, once again, this time with a fresh start and successful record here in the new market. When the next Regional Manager's position became available, I applied. Spencer, a Sales Manager who was formerly from the acquired bank, also applied. The interview panel consisted of Spencer's posse: his mentor, Frank; Lana, his next-door neighbor and also a Regional Manager; Tammy, who hired him; Yuri, the Market Manager; and Sara of Human Resources. All but Yuri had worked with, promoted, or hired Spencer. By this time, Tammy, who didn't know what a Sales Manager was, had now been promoted to be the Market Manager in charge of all Sales Managers. I'm sure they'll make her successful. I guess that made perfect sense since, as she told the story, she got her start in banking because her future father-in-law saw her walking down the street and told her to come into the bank the next day to start working. Once again, I was told I was the top candidate, blah, blah, blah. I'd heard it all before. Spencer was given the position.

Unpaid Dues

The sacrifice of leaving my family and home was not paying off. The hiring practices were much the same in the South as they were in the North. I was defeated and powerless. A Regional Manager's position with Dave Rummage became available in my old market. I applied. *The devil you know is better than the one you don't know.* This was at least an opportunity to get back home and be with my family.

Now with my additional success in another market, I applied and sent Dave a letter for consideration. In the letter, I shared the successes and accomplishments I'd had in the new market and the value I could bring back to his market. Dave never responded. He hired another privileged man.

My family and friends had no idea how depressed I was. They all saw me as strong and able to just do it. I am their measure of success. I couldn't really talk to anyone about it. If I brought it up, the response was always the same:"You got this, you can do it," and then they would just go on to talk about whatever issue they needed me to resolve for them.

As close as Maurier and I were, I couldn't talk to him because it felt like he was punishing me for moving, and I felt like I was proving his point. Therefore, I tried not to discuss my feelings with him, either. Still pushing my feelings and needs away, *old habits die hard.*

Yuri asked me to strongly consider applying for Spencer's former position of Sales Manager and support him as the new Regional Manager. I said emphatically, "NO! I've already proven myself and have no reason to believe that this would help me get a Regional Manager's position."

She explained that the bank needed to see me in leadership roles outside of the branch. Yuri was the only Market Manager who explained the necessity of how this move could *possibly* lead me on the path to Regional Manager. Though in my experience with this bank, this wasn't the necessary path for my White counterparts, her explanation was perhaps a plausible opportunity for me to become a Regional Manager. I applied and was hired.

To be eligible for a relocation stipend, the distance had to be at least four hours. This relocation for me was five hours. However, when I asked for the stipend, it was denied. My desperation was recognized and taken advantage of at every opportunity.

Sales Manager

Spencer was a natural complainer, and I'm sure he went to Tammy —now my manager—to complain about how he didn't want me to make him look bad in front of his staff. Tammy called me in for a meeting to "discuss my role as Sales Manager." For kicks and giggles, I played the game, pretending she knew what she was talking about. The meeting turned out to instead be her admonishing me in her Southern drawl, "Now Darlene, we know you have more "skeels" (skills) and knowledge about the Regional Manager's position than Spencer, but ya (your) job is to support him and make him look good and not make him feel embarrassed."

Now I had to make the White man feel superior. What kind of fucking alternate universe was this, where a company makes it very comfortable and acceptable for folks to *tell* you that they know you have what it takes to do the job but will give it to their friends and expect you to do the job for them?

Spencer was the epitome of a young White guy who got all his positions not because he earned them but because he was a young White guy, six feet tall and blond, with a family to take care of—*we'll just act like the year is 1787 and Black people are only "3/5ths human" and didn't have families. Right.* He just got pushed right up the proverbial "corporate ladder." He was a talker and loved to talk about how Frank, his mentor, pushed him into opportunities, how Tammy hired and promoted him, and how Lana was his next-door neighbor and good friend. So it was no surprise when he boasted about his second marriage to a much younger woman.

Behind his back, the whole region knew and told the story of him cheating on his first wife with his now second wife. He liked telling us about how his new, young wife idolized him because he had a big pension account from the old company, and she was so amazed that they had "all this money." He drove his yellow sports convertible and bragged to his staff and anyone who would listen about how he spent his weekends walking around the malls with his buzz cut and his gun on his hip so that everyone could think he was a cop. *God, what a blowhard.* As I observed him at meetings and on branch visits, he proved to be absolutely clueless about the responsibility of the job. He wouldn't even discipline one manager because she let him and his family use her beachfront house every summer. Nepotism ran deep at this bank, and it was repulsive.

Within the next six months, Yuri continued to quasi-support me from a distance. She nominated me to be one of only eighteen Sales Managers in the company to work with a consulting group to implement a new company-wide sales initiative. Our responsibility was to train all Branch Managers and Sales employees throughout the company. This assignment gave all of us direct contact and exposure to the top executives of the company. The folks whose names you see on letterhead but never cross paths with. We met with them regularly to have round table discussions about the progress of the initiative, and they knew and recognized us by name.

We traveled throughout the company from Florida to Pennsylvania to Ohio and everywhere in between. We were flying, driving, and staying at hotels in different states every week. We never knew where we would be assigned the following week, and received our assignments on the Sunday before we were to travel. There was no rhyme or reason for the assigned locations, and since this determined our mode of transportation, more times than not we would drive due to the untimely notification of our next assignments. I got a lot of windshield time, sometimes finding myself driving from the easternmost shores of North Carolina to the westernmost parts of Pennsylvania. The project lasted eighteen months. We were told that due to our participation in this project, at its completion, we would be the first to be considered for promotional opportunities and could cherry-pick where we'd like to go in the company. I was sure this would be the push I needed to become a Regional Manager. Most of my peers on this project did move on to become a part of the senior management team in some capacity. I went back to being the Sales Manager for Spencer.

When I returned from the assignment, my span of control as Sales Manager was increased from covering fifteen branches in Spencer's region to supporting twenty-eight branches, now including Lana's (Spencer's neighbor) region. I facilitated regular monthly meetings for the two regions and certified sixty-seven Branch Managers and Sales employees under the new sales initiative.

Yuri nominated me for a Circle of Excellence Award (only given to the top five percent of employees in the company), and she also gave me a Market All-Star Award.

Shortly after I returned, Lana was terminated, and I applied for her position. Yuri chose me as the candidate that she presented to Robert—her boss. I was elated. Finally the chosen candidate for a Regional Manager's position. One more hurdle. I still had my interview with her manager, Robert Thompson (yes, Dave Rummage's boss and Territory Manager for the Eastern part of the company).

Brad also applied for the position but was told he was not performing in the Sales Manager's role and was also not Regional Manager material. Redheaded Paul from the Bank at Work Program was terminated, and Brad was "transferred" (promoted) to be the Bank at Work Market Manager to replace Paul. As I continued to experience, this was the accepted culture of this bank. White men get promoted when they can't perform, and White women get the "we'll make you successful" tap on the shoulder. This place was like a game of musical chairs for the privileged.

This time I would try to play "politics." I'd talk to my manager, clueless Tammy, notify her of my application, and follow the chain of command, giving her the benefit of the doubt; after all, she was in all the Market Meetings with Robert. She should be able to give me some key pointers to discuss during the interview.

I was scheduled for a telephone interview with Robert. Of course, Tammy had steered me down the wrong path, and I believe Robert thought I was a complete idiot. It was a disaster. My saving grace was that Robert's secretary screwed up and scheduled us for a telephone interview instead of a face-to-face. Yuri called me and said after revisiting my application with Robert and having a lot more conversation about why I was the right candidate, she was able to get me scheduled for a second interview with Robert, and that it was important for me to be myself.

Robert started the interview by saying, "I've had one bad experience when interviewing someone on the phone, and from then on I decided to never again conduct a phone interview. I'll start by saying that I don't remember anything from the telephone interview, so this is a clean slate. Let's get started." I was thankful for his kindness and the opportunity to reset.

The interview went well. We had good banter and flow in the conversation about my career and what I would bring to the territory as a Regional Manager. However, I was disappointed that Robert didn't remember meeting me at E'Berg where I waited outside with him for his car, and we'd discussed my future goals. He told me to reach out to him when I was ready to relocate. Despite my many successes in the Northeast market, I was apparently just another faceless Branch Manager in the sea of many.

Yuri was right; just being myself sans Tammy's information made me more relaxed and confident.

I went through an additional three-month process of panel interviews. After five months into the process, I considered the blunders of the telephone interview with Robert and concluded that I would not get the job. Maurier and I decided to move forward with the building of our new home in the South. One week after we signed our contract with the builder, I was notified that I got the job of Regional Manager. It took ten years—2005 to 2015—two major banks, nine interviews, across four states, enduring the expense of moving four times within three years, fighting through prejudices and other obstacles, and working harder than any of my peers ever had to. I got it. I finally achieved my goal of becoming a Regional Manager. It was also the beginning of a five-year illness for my mother.

12
Maturity Date

My sister Deborah called to say Mommy was in the hospital and in a coma. Although new to my position, I dropped everything. In addition to my already hectic travel schedule for work and my personal life, I now added additional flights to include taking care of my mother. I got a flight, drove to the airport, jumped on a plane, and went to New York—more times than I could count. After several days, the doctors said they could not explain it. They didn't know why she was comatose. She was transferred to another hospital specializing in head traumas. This coma lasted a few weeks, and then she woke up with no explanation as to what happened. She was transferred to a rehabilitation center for eight weeks and returned home.

Meanwhile, Yuri and Sara, the Human Resources Representative, said I needed to live in the region. Just another obstacle that no other Regional Manager had to adhere to. I recognized it for what it was, but in my desperation to be a Regional Manager, I was not going to let this stop me. So, I relocated yet again and found a rental in my region, three hours away from my new home. I now had the house in Pennsylvania on the market for sale, my new home, the rental I had as Sales Manager, and now the rental I was mandated to have in my region as a condition of my being a Regional Manager. My monthly expenses for mortgages and rent were more than I was bringing home in my paycheck. Thank God Maurier's business was now well established because I was now paying for the promotion that I had rightfully earned. My landlord for the rental I'd had as a Sales Manager allowed me to break the lease with a one-month penalty. I was not surprised when, once again, my request for a relocation stipend was denied. I had no work-life balance outside of my car except for the regular flights to get the Pennsylvania house ready for sale, visit Maurier, and check on Mommy's health. When not flying, I drove the three hours home on Friday evenings, grabbed dinner from some fast food place, and then drove back to the region on Sunday evenings to start my week of driving five hundred miles to visit my branches.

To my detriment, two months into my new position, Yuri was transferred to another area of the bank. She was replaced by Jennifer, an Event Coordinator for the territory. Jennifer lasted a few months. I cannot speak to an Event Coordinator's experience in running the market, but as I continued to experience here, for the privileged, it was a normal occurrence to be promoted into positions of which you had no knowledge. Jennifer appeared quiet, meek even, and very soft-spoken. She never quite acclimated to the Market Manager's role. She was trying to manage the market while living in another state because her fifteen-year-old daughter refused to move—her words. I'm not familiar with a world where the child dictates to the parent what they will or will not do, especially when it impacts the family's livelihood. Logically, if she couldn't manage her fifteen-year-old daughter, how would she manage an entire market with over a thousand employees? She was a nice lady, but it was just as well that she left. Robert allowed her to go back to her old position, and he brought in Dana Dawson.

The Shit Show Began

Dana came in right about the time our annual reviews were to be delivered. Though no longer in the market, Yuri and Jennifer were responsible for completing our reviews, and Dana delivered them. When she met with me to give me my review, Dana emphatically confirmed that she had nothing to do with the content of my review and that she was only the messenger.

My review stated that I met all expectations, and it came with a *one* percent salary increase and a $9,900 stock option attached with the condition that I stay with the company for the next three years. I guess that this was somehow representative of the $10,000 pay cut I had to take three years prior when I relocated to the South. My displeasure showed on my face. I was not appeased or impressed. *This is total bullshit.*

Sitting at the table in the back of the little Italian restaurant, Dana reminded me once again that she was only the messenger of the review and that she "recognized that my salary was below par and that she was committed to bringing it into alignment." Dana then asked how she could help support my growth. I told her I would like to participate in the Women's Leadership Development Program as well as any other leadership programs the company offered, and I also wanted to participate in some of her market initiatives.

Dana said she was not familiar with the Women's Leadership Development program, but it sounded like something that she herself also needed to partake in. She also committed to making sure to get me on some of her market projects when they were available. We discussed our mutual bottom-line goals, and we committed to working together to reach these. As a new Regional Manager, I shared that now having had three Market Managers in less than a year, I was looking forward to her coaching and support as I got acclimated. She agreed. I also gave her some background information about the direction my career had taken, and that I was looking forward to future growth opportunities. I committed to being a strong contributor to her team in order for her to reach her goals. I kept up my end of that commitment. Dana's proved to be empty platitudes.

13
Reflections of Wisdom

Experience, societal and familial, has taught me that money, power, boundaries, and connections are the only true power sources that fuel success. The connections others are born into, I had to earn and learn, hoping that someone in power was liberal or compassionate enough to take me under their wing. In my observation, this sometimes happens for a person of color from another country, but it is very uncommon for a Black person in America. We rarely if ever have a daddy who went to school with the CEO of a company and can call him up and say my son or daughter needs a job. We are often busy struggling to survive day to day, and in my generation—although not so in my case, my dad completed his master-level education—more often than not the first person to complete or attend college. Additionally, to our detriment, many successful Black people don't reach out to help other Blacks for fear of being ostracized by their White counterparts or being seen as someone who is colorizing the company. Or they have the attitude of I got mine, you get yours (crabs in the barrel mentality). I didn't want to be like that.

I know some very talented people come from the most depressed communities, and I made sure I was observant and intentional when searching for talent to identify as many people of color, with potential, to help them get a start and move them into leadership positions. My rule of thumb is that the only time that I would look down on someone is when I'm reaching to give them a hand up. Knowing that no one else would, I made sure I did.

Fortunately, education and leadership are easy for me; unfortunately, no one taught me how to make connections. I didn't learn to linger at the water cooler after a meeting to chit-chat and gossip about people's families and pets. I didn't understand that these connections were where the deals were being made. Instead, I took away the directives, goals, and tasks assigned to me at the meeting and focused on achieving them. I believed being successful was measured by attaining tangible goals, following the rules, excelling, being dependable, and leading the way. I didn't realize I had already missed the prize because the promotions were already made at the water coolers and on the golf courses where people were connecting. I was never in any of those places.

My Blackness, coupled with the lessons taught at home, left me powerless against the games of the world.

PART III: UNBANKED

14
Compliance Risk

Dana's opening statement and introduction at our first Regional Manager's meeting was, "Your other manager couldn't cut it, but I am here to stay." Her next line was, "I always get my way. Even at home when my husband says that he doesn't work for me, I keep pushing until he gives in."

Dana was cocky and liked boasting publicly about how she destroyed someone's career and/or life. Her style was to build up an employee's confidence and then systematically go about destroying that person's life and career. She thrived on it.

Fortunately, I had witnessed the "Mean Girls of the South" (Dana, Sara from HR, and Stacey from operations), as they were not so affectionately known. When they identified a target, their goal was to systematically force the person out of the company, their career, and their livelihood. At Dana's request, Sara and Stacey would gather and manipulate data to create false outcomes for their targeted victim. Having witnessed their behavior, I recognized immediately when I had become Dana's target. I had a second phone and started recording as many calls with them and other management partners as possible.

Dana once told me she was frustrated with me because she didn't know what drove me and that I cared too much for my people. In other words, she wanted to know what my pain points were—my Achilles heel. Unbeknownst to her, while worrying herself about finding my Achilles heel (pain points), she had already identified it. *I cared too much for my people. In business and my personal life. Where I can, I will always stand in the way of protecting their rights and protecting them from harm.*

Things went downhill from here.

The Downward Trend

Dana had a market-wide business development challenge. We were to get together with our Business and Investment Peer Partners and go out jointly on a Saturday. The goal was to encourage referrals and present ourselves as partners and support teams for the branch staff. It was either not communicated or not well received by our Business Partners, or I missed the memo. None of the partners came out, and very few Regional Managers participated.

At our next Regional Manager's meeting, Dana was discussing the event as if it were successful, and she discussed having another such event. I said it was important for us to confirm that the partners were on board since they did not show up for the last event. Otherwise, we are just wasting time. Dana did an exorcist turn of her neck to look at me. She was pissed, and pissed Dana was vindictive Dana with a laser focus on destroying her target while mowing down everything in her way. She was clearly angry that I stated the obvious. *I thought this was an open discussion? How dare I state the obvious?* I put a bullseye on my head.

Later that week, at our one-on-one meeting, I told Dana I would like to take some of the training classes offered to employees and that I also needed to start managing my work-life balance better. Again, constantly searching for ways to harm me, Dana now believed that she had identified my Achilles heel.

The words had barely left my mouth when she said, "If you need a better work-life balance that bad, I can demote you back down to a Sales Manager." Astonished was not the word. I had heard Dana say some pretty foul things, but this was low and unnecessary. If my jaw could hit the floor, it would have landed with a loud clink—teeth rattle and all.

I'd put in countless and continuous hours day in and day out. My marriage was on the brink, I had no personal life, and only God knows what was going on with my health. And *the best* she could offer me was a threat of a demotion? I know what it means to feel undervalued, but this was a new level of low. She didn't even take the time to fake it like she cared. That was the devil I was used to. Dana was a different type of ruthless. Like a shark in the water with the scent of blood, she made me her next target and started her systematic assault on me.

Blind-Sided and Set Up for Failure

According to the United States national statistics, my region included the largest geographic territory in the state and had the lowest per capita income. Dana started her attack on me by giving me the second most aggressive goal in the market. Despite the discriminatory and inequitable manner they were distributed (according to the bank's standards of per capita opportunity) Dana and Sara acknowledged I was the second-highest contributor to the market's overall sales.

Consistently outperforming my peers, my "reward" was later announced. Dana notified me that because of my leadership, skills, and talent, she was able to restructure the market and increase my span of control by adding six additional branches to my region. I guess my facial expression was waiting for the punchline and the revealing of the reward because Dana followed up with, "Now, Darlene, this is a good thing. I would not be able to do this if it wasn't for your abilities."

Sara was on the sideline in her usual bobblehead manner, nodding her head in the affirmative to anything Dana. In addition to my commute, my drive time now spanned as far north as the northern border of the state, as far east as the Atlantic Ocean, and as far south and just shy of the southern border state, and various towns and cities along the way. My head was spinning as fast as the wheels on my car driving down I-95 and every rural highway and byway in between. My friends were worried about all the time I spent on the road and took turns calling me when I was driving to keep me company. I appreciated their care, but I had no time to be concerned for myself. It didn't really cross my mind. It was a part of the cost to live the dream I longed for. Travel became my truest companion.

I worked my ass off. We decreased our losses and moved from becoming the worst region in the market to one of the top three performing regions. We were the second largest contributor to overall sales with the lowest Sales employee turnover.

However, my dream of becoming a Regional Manager was quickly becoming a nightmare. I was under attack by Dana and the "Mean Girls of the South," my marriage felt like it was unraveling, and my mother was extremely sick, and unbeknownst to me, slowly dying.

When the Mean Girls had you in their crosshairs, they did everything they could to force you to quit, and they made life hell for you. It was the most extreme case of the "Horn Effect" you can imagine because you were punished based on what Dana deemed was your most recent offense. I was subjected to calls on which Dana would send me an agenda, and she would change it on the call. Knowing I had prepared for the call based on her agenda, Dana would say, "We're not talking about that now."

On one weekly call with our partners, Dana was in full bully mode, and I was her victim. There were ten other people—her peers—on the call when she went in on me. Her dauntingness was persistent. Nothing I said was right, and she was single-minded and more vicious than usual in her blood-thirsty pursuit.

She started with "Well, Darlene, you said you want to win. Tell me how you are going to win." I started to explain my course of action—she'd cut me off—taunting me by saying, "Well you want to win, you want to win, tell me how you're going to win? What are you going to do?" I would start again—she'd cut me off again—"You want to win, so what are you going to do?" She was the bully poking me constantly in my chest, screaming in my face, with each rant getting more erratic with every poke to my chest. "Tell me what you're going to do. Tell me what you're going to do; you want to win; tell me what you're going to do."

I finally said, "Dana, I'm not quite sure what you expect me to say, but I don't have anything else to add." She kept up her tirade, ranting and raving. The schoolyard bully poking and poking, screaming through the phone. She ranted on and on for about fifteen minutes—she was clearly unraveling. I was the victim, and the schoolyard bully had an audience. It got so bad that her peers began sending me text messages asking if I was okay and what I did to her. I responded to some of the texts that I was not sure what was going on or why she was behaving like this. I hadn't done anything.

Dana finally said, "If you really want to win, you would get on the phone right now and call all of your managers and demand that they each open a new bank account today for the next customer that comes into the branch."

It was 4:50 p.m. on the last day of the month. Corporate bullies always have a way of knowing how to disguise their intimidation tactics in HR-approved lingo.

As she continued her rant, I thought, *Is this the bank I work for, or is this the other well-known bank that was being sued and sanctioned by the banking commission for illegal practices of opening accounts for customers without their permission?* Here she was, at 4:50 p.m. on the last day of the month, demanding that I commit the same illegal practice to meet her goal. *Is her coaching/demand really that I call my nineteen Branch Managers and demand they illegally open an account before five o'clock? Was anyone else even listening to these illegal demands?* I knew that even if they were, no one would ever say anything because they knew she would target them next. It was a shit show for sure.

Market Depreciation

Each week, Dana identified her target, and although they knew Dana had crossed the line, the other two members of the Mean Girls (Sara and Stacey) gathered and manipulated information to fuel Dana's fire. Dana would attack her target, and when she had an audience, you could visualize her beating her chest and ranting, "I'll get them; just watch me." When the person quit, she would send out a text and say, "I told you I would get them because if they don't do what I say, I'll call their boss and make something happen."

If you filed a complaint, Sara would instead pull up your entire work history and use anything she could find against you to make you look like the offender. She would use your previous conversations with her, your words, and your work history to defend Dana. You never knew on the call who Dana was going to attack, but you could be sure she had an agenda. We were like mice scurrying from a cat, and when she cornered one, you could hear the inflection in her voice and imagine her on the other end telling her cronies, "*I'll get her. I'll get her.* Just watch."

I watched her destroy careers regularly—people who had been around for thirty and even forty years. Her favorite mantra was, "Oh I'll get them because if they don't respond to me, I'll call their boss, and Robert Thompson will back me up." She constantly said, "I love Robert. He always has my back. He'll always watch out for me."

With her office down the hall from his, Dana certainly had immediate access to Robert's ear; however, it made you wonder about the professionalism of their relationship. It was as if Robert was giving her the green light to bully anyone in the market. Dana was a cancer in the market —eating up all the weaker cells around her, surrounding herself with all the weak people who would not speak up—people who quietly and silently stood by. Afraid of her wrath, their silence demonstrated their complicit support of her behavior.

Gary—her Business Banking Partner—resigned, throwing away his forty-year career by stating she was impossible, and he could no longer work with her. He was under constant attack from her. She was regularly reporting him to his manager—Robert's peer.

Tammy—thirty-year career—was fired or forced to resign. Dana sent me a text reading, "GOT HER. I told you that I would get her." I still have the text. She did not care who witnessed her tirades and was clearly unconcerned about any repercussions.

When visiting her office one day for a face-to-face meeting with her and Sara, she had apparently sent her secretary Bonnie out to get her lunch. Bonnie came into the conference room where we were meeting and gave her the salad. She opened it and started yelling like a two-year-old, just short of banging her utensils on the table, right in the conference room with Sara and me. "What is she, a fucking idiot? How many times do I have to say I don't eat meat?" Bonnie had to hear her. Now screaming at a screeching octave, "Why is there chicken on my salad?" It was like watching the Joan Crawford movie *Mommy Dearest* when she was screaming, "No wire hangers!"

She was so unhinged that "Mean Girl" Stacey came running into the conference room and said, "I'll go and get you another one." Sara said nothing, just glancing from me to Dana as if trying to silently remind Dana that I was in the room. Bonnie quit the next week—her thirty-five-year career down the drain. Bonnie was Sara's friend. The backstabbing was deep. No one was spared from Dana's wrath.

Dana kept you off your axis because, like any bully, when she was in person without an audience, when it was just the two of us, she would use this sickening sing-song voice. "Hi, Darlene! How are you?" and then she would hug me. Dana was skilled at switching between her representational self and her true self on a whim to suit her fancy. Her nice act was so obviously different from who she actually was that it was insulting that she would believe others perceived her as anything *other* than vile. It was perfectly like Dana to be insulting, even when trying to put on the *façade* of being nice. Calling her mean was a compliment on the right day.

15
Unexpected Withdrawals

Mommy

I received a call from my sister, Deborah, saying Mommy was back in the hospital. She had once again fallen into this mysterious coma. While my sister visited and sat with Mommy for endless hours, sometimes eighteen hours or more, she couldn't or wouldn't make any decisions. She always deferred to me and told the doctors they had to talk to her big sister. She believes that, as the oldest, my role is to make the decisions. My whole family refers to me as the business head. I don't think it's negative, but it does add a lot of responsibility.

I flew up to sign any paperwork and manage any decisions. This time the doctors tried to do a spinal tap. I became concerned that the doctor was treating her as if she was a cadaver. One day they examined her in the intensive care unit, and when we came to visit, she was lying naked in the bed—no gown, no blanket, right in front of the nurses' station. They literally left her lying naked after they did their examination. There was no diagnosis. One doctor would say a stroke, the next would say there was no evidence of a stroke. She woke up, was sent to rehab and then back home.

I was so stressed with all the things pulling me in different directions. It wasn't enough that I felt like I lived to travel, but the demand was intense when I showed up to whatever scene needed me next. I was living in such a perpetual state of "big girl" and "get it done" that overwhelmed became my normal blood pressure. Between my marriage, my mother, my branches, and Dana, I was exhausted beyond what my body or mind could fathom.

16
Overdrawn

Resources Withheld

November was the start of a very bad dream, but I knew little of what the witch was brewing up behind the scenes for me. It was about November when I first became Dana's target. She started systematically withholding resources from me. I was officially under attack by the "Mean Girls of the South." Dana's attacks were consistent and methodical.

Two-Legged Stool

Dana decided to build strong relationships with the Operations team. The Regional Managers were to host a weekly call with our Sales Manager and our Operational Peer Partner—-who reported to "Mean Girl Stacey." The strategy was to identify gaps or weaknesses within operations at the branch level to mitigate risk and then implement change and shore things up during our weekly branch visits. These were called the three-legged stool meetings. We, the Regional Manager, Operations Partner, and Sales Manager, each represented a leg on a stool.

After three weeks, Dana scheduled a call and said that my Sales Manager was no longer allowed on my call. No explanation was given. *I was now the "two-legged" stool in the market, clearly unable to stand.* My Operations Partner, Brenda, told me I was the only Regional Manager who was not allowed to have their Sales Manager resource on their calls. Dana's goal was to make me fall and fail hard, however you looked at it.

This created extra meetings and communication breakdowns for me. Not having my Sales Manager on these calls meant I now had to host two additional weekly meetings—one before the call to get pertinent information my Sales Manager had gathered during her branch visits, and then I would share and disseminate that information on my two-legged stool call with my Operations Partner. She and I would then develop a course of action for the following week. I would then have a second meeting with my Sales Manager to disseminate the plan to make sure the three of us were on the same page.

By now I viewed every attack on me as discriminatory in more ways than one, and being the only person of color just magnified my experience. Dana continually harassed me and withheld resources from me and didn't stop there. Unfortunately, I had not recorded this meeting where Brenda first disclosed that I was being singled out. So I set her up. I knew it would be easy.

Brenda was smart, like a bag of hammers. She was always looking for gossip and loved sharing information as if she were in the know. I asked her to inquire at her next meeting with Stacey and Dana if my Sales Manager could rejoin our three-legged stool meetings. At our next week's meeting—now recording her—I asked Brenda what Dana's answer was. Brenda said, "Dana leads our meetings, and she said that your Sales Manager is still not allowed on your three-legged stool call. Stacey and I are waiting for Dana to give us the go-ahead to allow your Sales Manager to rejoin the call." It never happened.

On my weekly call with Dana, she told me she was managing and coaching Stacey because Stacey was incapable of making decisions. This just further confirmed for me that Brenda was right, and Dana was pulling all the strings. I tried my best to keep showing up to the fight.

Reducing Fee Refunds

It was becoming more and more abundantly clear that Dana was just making shit up to harass me. As we continued to shore things up in Operations, Dana told me to speak to Brandin, another Regional Manager, about strategies for improving fee refunds "because Brandin was a clear communicator who drove consistent expectations and achieved the expected results regarding fee refunds." I recognized the torment for what it was. Brandin was in second place in the market. I was number one in this area. It was these kinds of demands that did not make sense, as if Dana wasn't even looking at the data, but instead, her goal was to keep me under attack to see if she could break me.

It never dawned on me that these persistent attacks were taking the toll on me that they were. I was so focused on hitting goals and meeting the outrageous demands that I never considered the amount of energy I placed into keeping up with her crazy. Perhaps if I had been more aware, maybe I would have considered another course of action, but I had tunnel vision and had worked too hard to get the role of Regional Manager to let a bully push me out. The Mean Girls had nothing on the years of mean that I had already experienced by White women in corporate and from neglect at home. I was not about to back down.

Safety Risk

In December, the bank announced it was closing some of its branches. The affected Regional Managers were emailed instructions, followed up by a call with Dana and Sara. It was the Regional Manager's responsibility to notify the branch employees. We were given a script to follow and a week to meet with the affected branch employees. Our delivery was to be in person to the branch staff, followed immediately by one-on-one meetings with each employee in the branch to answer questions, hear their thoughts, deal with their emotions, and explain the next steps. On my call, Dana said, "There are three branches in your region that will be closing. I want them all notified tomorrow." Friday.

I said, "Dana, this would entail me visiting three branches, meeting with and coaching each Branch Manager on how to positively navigate through this, then meeting one-on-one with each branch employee, allowing each employee a minimum of thirty minutes for discussion, and then driving to the next branch to do the same. A total of eighteen employees. Not only is this emotionally draining, but it is also at least a two-hundred-mile drive for me to get them all done in one day."

Dana said, "I don't care; I want them all done tomorrow."

I reminded her that the guidelines said we had a week to deliver the information to the branches and asked her if it would be okay if I did one branch each on Friday, Monday, and Tuesday, allowing the employees time to digest the information and me time to drive safely. She reiterated, this time raising her voice, "I want them all done tomorrow, and you are to call me when you get to the first branch and put me on speaker because I don't believe you will deliver the information objectively!" Sara, also on the call, said nothing. I never expected Sara to speak up. She was always too busy bowing down to Dana, but today of all days it would have meant the most.

This was cruel and unusual punishment, and I had no choice but to comply. However, and more importantly, Dana purposely put my safety at risk. Simply getting to the branches within the day was enough for any person. Besides, people needed time to process losing their jobs. The script was not enough for the emotion that comes with the devastating news, and in typical Dana fashion, she had no regard for anyone or anything except her goal of destruction. She needed a reason to break me, and I just wasn't going to give her one. I grabbed breakfast for the branch and arrived in the parking lot of the first branch—fifty miles from home—at 7:30 a.m.

I notified the team that Sara and Dana would be on the call. I dialed Dana and Sara in at 8:00 a.m. and made the announcement to the staff. Sara and Dana hung up, never making any comments to the staff. I then set myself up in an office and met with each employee to answer the obvious questions. Understanding that losing a job is one of the top stressors a person can have in life, I was not going to let the abuse that I was getting from Dana trickle down to them. I was not going to treat them like cattle by rushing them through the process.

The questions were obvious, emotional, and time-consuming, as each employee processed the information differently. *Am I going to lose my job? Will I be relocated to a branch close to my home?* All eighteen employees. On and on, and then I was off to the next branch. I was in shock, numb, and weighted down a little more after each conversation, processing and bearing the grief of each employee.

Covering the two-hundred-mile span, I drove eighty-five miles an hour down I-95 to I-64, through the corn fields, and across bridges to meet Dana's demands. Pushing myself to inhuman limits, I had no time to eat. I just kept on task, pushing from one employee to the other. It was 6:30 p.m., eleven hours later, when my last employee meeting ended. I called Dana to let her know I had finished. She didn't answer, so I left her a voice message. However, seconds later, before I could disconnect, Sara was calling. She asked if I was okay—once again protecting Dana and her antics. It was obvious that they were together. My energy was completely overdrawn and depleted. I was exhausted. Now ahead of me, with eyes drooping and stomach in knots, I had my three-hour drive home.

What I later learned was that I was the only Regional Manager told to make these announcements on that day and that there was only one other branch that was being closed in our market. Dana allowed that Regional Manager the entire week to decide when he would notify his branch. Dana purposely put my life in danger

17
Progressive Tax

As the bank continued to make adjustments to compete for talent in the industry, it was highly recommended that managers take the Myers-Briggs class offered by the bank. This class led to other classes that were offered. I scheduled some additional classes where my schedule allowed. *It couldn't hurt.* In the interim, Dana rescheduled one of her standing meetings, and the new date conflicted with the time of one of my classes. The class ended at noon, and my travel time would have been about an hour. Her meeting started at noon. I asked Dana if she would be okay with me arriving an hour later to the meeting. She said no! Of course.

Canceling my class, I arrived at the meeting only to find that she was having a holiday luncheon from noon to one, and the actual meeting would start at one. I canceled my class to have dry bagel sandwiches with a group of peers who didn't even talk to me. Dana was driving the nails into my coffin at every opportunity. She was doing anything and everything to destroy me.

I continued to seek out resources tenaciously. As a bank advocate for women in business, it made sense to me that I hone my skills by attending the Women's Leadership and Development Program. To attend, approvals from your Market Manager and Market Human Resources Partner (Dana and Sara) had to be submitted in November for the January session. Notifications about the program went to the Market Managers in September. I continually asked Dana and Sara about submitting approval for me to attend. Dana kept saying she never received the September notice, but to keep checking. I was relentless and inquired every week on our one-on-one calls about her receipt of the notification. She continued to say she hadn't gotten the request for submission. However, when I asked Sara in late November, she replied, "I think you should ask Dana again." I believe Sara knew that Dana had received the information. Dana, however, continued to insist she hadn't heard anything.

Finally, during one call when I asked Dana , she said the company had not made a decision yet. *Oh, so you did receive it. I guess she forgot her own lies.* Of course, I had done my research, so I knew this was Dana's decision. It was never the bank's. Once again—like any bully without an audience—she was cowardly hiding behind the company.

Over the next four months, I continued to ask about the Women's Leadership Program, and finally, in March, when the January session was well on its way, Dana told me I was not selected for the Program. I reminded her that there were four sessions per year. She told me I was not selected for any of them. The sessions are only approved one at a time—two months before the start of each new session. Dana had already decided she would never consider me for the program. I'm sure to Dana and the Mean Girls' chagrin, I was determined to continue my course and successfully meet my goals.

Non-Compensation

In the meantime, salary reviews and recommendations for increases are also decided in November to be communicated by the end of February, and any increase would be reflected in the first paycheck of March. During the review period, Sara called me several times asking me to increase the salary recommendations for my employees. She explained that the market had too much money in its budget and needed all Regional Managers to take a second look at each employee's salary. Sara went down the list of each employee, asking me to revisit any employee not on corrective action and to put them in for an increase sans their performance.

Dana had skimmed increases down so much that she now had a deficit in what she was expected to budget for salary increases. At this point, they were not even looking at performance.

At the same time, the bank was losing out on good talent because of their low salary levels. As a result, they increased salaries in every retail job family to be competitive with other banks. A part of this strategy included full disclosure and transparency of salaries in all job families. This is how I discovered that I was paid significantly less than my peers.

It never occurred to me to think about what the others made. Early in my career, we were open and transparent about what we made, and I never thought or considered I could get this far into my career to see a vast pay difference from the same job level. Despite this parity, the excess money in the budget, and my "acceptable performance," Dana refused to correct this. She was instead ranting and raving about her inability to know my "pain points"—Achilles heel. She cared more about knowing my vulnerabilities for her power-hungry, emotionally-controlling antics than simply doing her job. I had survived being overlooked for promotions because I wasn't "one of the privileged," to get promoted by the default of the relationship, but this was a new low of personal pursuit to my demise.

Despite the "excess in funds" and my "stellar performance," as per Dana and Sara on my weekly call (I recorded this conversation), Dana refused to give me a salary increase.

Dana called me at 5:00 p.m. on February 28th to tell me I would not be getting a salary increase. I said, "Considering my 'stellar performance' and contribution to the market, What is the basis of your decision?"

She said, "Let's have a call tomorrow with Sara."

We scheduled the call for the following day. After the normal cordiality of greetings, Dana started, "Sara, please explain to Darlene and me why she did not get a salary increase." *Dana, you decide who gets salary increases. Is she really cowardly hiding behind some made-up corporate BS?*

Sara started reading from some script that was clearly created for this call, never before heard by anyone in the market. "Behavioral execution elements that [I] drive business, which translates into performance outcomes, was the measure used at the senior levels to give salary increases." I asked what the behavioral elements were that she was citing. Sara proceeded to state six behavioral elements.

I felt my blood begin to boil. I said, "Of those six metrics you cited, I am the number one contributor in the market in four of them, and second and third in the other two. What would be the deciding factor if not for a top performer in all of these metrics?"

Sara said, "Darlene, you had an exceptional performance; however, everyone could not get a raise." I hung up, not caring what the repercussions would be. Things couldn't get any worse. *Or so I thought.*

Mommy

My mother returned to the hospital again and again. In the hospital, into rehab, and back home. To my dismay, this cycle continued, and I'm sure to hers, too.

One Saturday, Deborah called me crying hysterically, barely able to relay the message. "Darlene, this doctor here said that anybody who wants to see Mommy better come now because she isn't going to make it."

I said, "Let me speak to the doctor." When I did, he suggested I get there as soon as possible.

I called the airline and got the next flight out. When I got to the hospital, it turned out the doctor was wrong. *Thank God.* The head doctor was there, and he said at this time, your mother's death is not imminent.

The doctor who sounded the alarm was standing there but said nothing. When I confronted him, he said, "Well, I didn't say she was going to die. I just said you needed to come right away." I reminded him how he told my sister the same thing. If you tell someone this is the last time they have an opportunity to see a loved one, the natural thought is that the person is dying. He was removed from my mother's case, and rightfully so because who taught this man bedside manner?

During this hospital stay, they also tried to do a spinal tap, but Mommy had no fluid in her back. They must've tried five times while she was unconscious and finally gave up. When she woke up, they tried to do the spinal tap again. The doctors said they would not put her to sleep but would give her a local numbing agent.

From outside the room where the procedure was being done, I could hear Mommy crying and screaming in pain. Finally, I screamed through the door, "*Just stop!*" She was sent back to rehab. When I got back home a week later, I pulled into my driveway to see the rental car I used for my job—*oh shoot*. I had completely forgotten all about the rental car for work. So instead of submitting an expense report for that week, I paid out of pocket.

I was so consumed with caring for Mommy from a distance, traveling across my region, and ensuring I gave Maurier time, that I had no time or energy left for me. It was a hard season, but this "big girl" could do it. It was automatic to me, and as usual, I set my sight on autopilot (no pun intended) to get it done. After all, how else would it happen? I didn't see any other option. I lived under this premise for years, and my body started to show me that it was tired of carrying the weight.

More Tax

Shortly after returning from this stint with Mommy Sara called one morning with her manager, Lisa, also on the call. Sara started by saying, "Darlene, knowing that you rent cars, this is just to ask you some questions about how the rental policy works." *As if the Human Resources Retail and Market Manager doesn't know the rental car policy. But okay*

Sara started with, "How do you rent cars for work?" I told her the company's car rental policy is that if you drive more than one hundred miles per week, you can rent a car instead of using your personal car. Sara proceeded to ask me about every rental I had and where I picked the car up. I told her I picked the car up on Saturdays near my home because the rental company where the bank has its negotiated corporate rates is closed near me on Sundays.

I heard typing on the computer keys, and then Sara said, "That's right. I see they are closed on Sunday." *Aha, this is another witch hunt. She's verifying everything that I say.*

I continued. "This way, I have the car for my drive from home to the region on Sunday evenings. The mileage is free, and I pay for gas out of my pocket to refill and be prepared to start my work day on Monday. I rent the car monthly because it is the cheapest company-negotiated rate."

She then asked, "What did you do with the rental when you went to see your mother?" I told her the doctor said my mother wasn't going to make it, and in my haste to get to her, I left the rental in my driveway and paid out of my pocket for the days it was there.

"Oh, yes; I see that's when you paid the $700."

I said yes, confirming that she was testing me and that she had all my rental car information in front of her. She then said, "It would be best if going forward you waited to get to your region to rent the car." I said that this would preclude me from arriving at my branch visit on time on

Mondays since the car rental company in my region doesn't open until 9:00 a.m., and I need to be in my branch by 7:30 or 8:00.

Ignoring what I said, she told me again to start renting my cars in my region. The stupidity of it all was that the rental company gave us free mileage, so it didn't matter where I rented the car. The expense to the bank would be the same since I paid out of pocket for the gas to and from my region. So, now I was to drive my personal car to the region on Sunday night, pick up a rental car on Monday, pay a higher weekly rate, leave my car in the unsecured car rental lot, and be late visiting my branches. I knew this course of action would provide more ammunition for Dana to use in her ongoing assault against me. Recognizing the set-up, I said no problem. Sara then told me to keep this call to myself, insisting they were calling everyone who rents cars to find out their process. I said no problem.

18
The Black Cost

As I experienced it, racism at this bank was from the top down. In her opening speech at our company-wide Regional Manager's Forum, in her opening speech, Amy, the CEO of the Retail Bank, said she recognized that there was no diversity at the top of the company, and her goal was to change this. She then said, "I encourage all of you to take a risk and start hiring people who don't look like you." I'm sure to the White Regional Managers in the room, this was a good speech—if they were even listening.

I and my four Black colleagues in the company were astounded. She was actually saying out loud and in public that it was a risk to hire someone who was not White. One of my young, brave, Black colleagues challenged her and asked, "Are we hiring by someone's looks?"

Amy—back peddling—said, "No, I'm saying when you hire, step out of your comfort zone, because we all tend to use a strategy we are comfortable with during the hiring process." She then used herself as an example and said, "For instance, my manager stepped out of his comfort zone and gave me a [the] 'tap on the shoulder' when he gave me this promotion." And when she exclaimed her surprise to him, saying she didn't have a clue about this job, he told her not to worry, that she would be fine. *And that, my friends, is how it's done for the privileged class of fair-haired folks at this bank.*

My eyes were popping out of my head. This lady with her golden locks and blue eyes, *Chief Executive Officer* of the entire Retail Banking division of a major bank, literally made a public statement of racism and privilege to a room of one hundred of her subordinates. Can we be any more comfortable in our privilege? What in the absolute fuck are we doing?!!!

Two months later, when Amy had the opportunity to rectify her "observation of non-diversity at the top," she announced the new head of the company's Business Banking division—a woman who was her exact replica. *Oops!!!* It looked like she forgot to step out of her comfort zone and change her hiring strategy.

As My Luck Would Have It

My ex-Banker Jeffrey, who was given the Private Customer Team Leader position, was also a guest speaker at this Forum. Unless something spectacular like a lobotomy had happened in the past years, I couldn't imagine what he was an expert in. However, when he saw me, he said, "I still don't know how I got that job over you. I guess Stephen just likes me because he has put me up for several other promotions since then." I just love it when the privileged show such incredulity over their unearned fortunes.

The Black Cost of Diversity

Whenever I'm in a meeting, I try to sit on the opposite end and opposite side of the table from the person hosting the meeting. This gives me a vantage point to observe the unspoken communications between people. I would purposely always make a point to get to Dana's meetings early to see her facial expressions and how she nonverbally communicated with Sara and my peers.

When we returned from the Regional Manager's Forum with CEO Amy, Dana hosted our monthly market meeting. So here I was, sitting at the far left end of the conference table with Dana at the other end on the far right and Sara by her side. I should have been prepared but was thrown off of my three-inch pumps when Dana and Sara announced we were going to have a diversity and inclusion session and asked everyone except the Regional Managers to leave the room.

Dana then proceeded to go around the table, asking each of my seven peers—Sara taking notes—"What is diversity in our market?" Smirks sounded around the table—everyone intentionally avoiding eye contact with me—each one regurgitating what Amy said at the Regional Forum: "Diversity is taking a risk and hiring someone who doesn't look like me."

When Dana finally got around the table to me, she thanked everyone for their input, smiling smugly while nodding in the affirmative to Sara. "We will now resume the meeting and invite our partners back in."

Dana never asked me the question, and I was mortified. I didn't say anything. *Why didn't I speak up?* I was so angry and embarrassed that she would openly exclude me, but I was more upset with myself. Why did I let the meeting move forward? I was so taken aback that I didn't respond in time, and now I couldn't circle back to the moment. I was, once again, the kid on the playground with the bully poking me in the chest—*again and again*—and in this moment, I let them.

I would have shared that for me the goal is to interview a pool of qualified candidates and hire the best candidate for the position, which would in itself yield a diverse team. I never got to share it, and I am convinced it would not have mattered that day, at least certainly not at Dana's table.

Dana also had several opportunities to diversify the team, but she chose not to. Four of the six Regional Managers who were there when she came on board had left. Never had we experienced such an outgoing of managers at that level or any level. Usually, Regional Managers, even Branch Managers, were stable in their positions. Not here with Dana Dawson. She replaced all four positions with White women who had worked for her in the past: her Secretary, two Branch Managers, and a displaced Investment Banker. They all finally left as well.

Perpetual Expense

As the Regional Manager, I was expected to sign off with Human Resources on wrongful terminations and other disciplinary actions against employees. Reports of discrimination were swept under the rug, and then there would be retaliation. It was a very hostile work environment. Several reported incidents made me feel unsafe, and my hands were tied to help my employees. I often reflected on my first encounter with Cathy Danish— when I reported Janice—when she told me "the middle-aged White woman from the South didn't mean me any harm."

As luck would have it, Cathy Danish was assigned to be my Peer Human Resource Partner for my region. Cathy liked to terminate employees based on her perceived moral compass of honesty, while she was as dishonest as a four-dollar bill. Most of her statements, assessments, and decisions belied racial undertones, and she constantly defended the discriminatory behavior of her White colleagues.

My *Internal Vault*

Unless you reported an incident yourself, Regional Managers were not notified of a Human Resources investigation until it was well underway or completed.

There were numerous incidents of discrimination against people of color in my region, certainly too many to re-hash; however, there are three that will live in my internal vault forever.

Case One

Cathy called to notify me that there had been an ongoing investigation for one of my branches, and that she had interviewed the employees and was recommending the termination of three employees—*all Black*—-and putting the other employees—*all White*—-on warning.

She then went on to give me the details of the investigation.

Every employee in the branch, Black and White, admitted to cashing employee checks of a business client without proper identification. Cathy said that she was aware that this practice in this branch had been going on for more than twenty years and through three bank mergers.

As I listened, I told her it was clear she was only firing the Black employees. She said, "We're not terminating the Black Branch Manager, although as the manager he should have known what was going on, but we spared him."

Cathy defended her recommendation for termination, saying that she "deemed the Black employees dishonest," which is a terminable offense, because when she asked them about this practice they first said they did not know, but then retracted and said that this was how they were trained for this customer, but were too afraid to admit it when she first interrogated them.Cathy further stated that because the White employees were not afraid and admitted to the wrongdoing, their jobs were spared.

Man, I raised the roof on this blatant racist action. I complained up and down the Human Resources chain. As a result of my complaints, the Branch Manager and I were summoned to join a call with Cathy and her manager Lisa at 7:30 a.m. the following morning. *7:30 AM appears to be the time when threats were made. You cannot make this up.*

Bringing in senior management was an intimidation tactic the bank used when you disagreed or asked too many questions about a decision. I wanted to be there in person with the manager when we took the call. I drove to his branch early that morning, and we took the call in my car. The call was just for Lisa to show her support for Cathy's decision. Taking this call in person with the manager was a show of support and was as close as I could get to advocacy for people like me. I had experienced enough pain behind things I could not change (my skin color and gender) and was limited on the support I could provide to do this for others who looked like me. It was a weighty and uphill battle.

Case Two

Carmen, a Hispanic Banker, put in a complaint with me that her manager, Lucille—another Southern White lady and long-time colleague of Cathy's— had instructed her to falsify her timesheet, and that no matter what time she went to lunch, she was to indicate on her time sheet that she took an hour. And "even if she left after one o'clock, she must return at 2:00 p.m. and must enter her time as leaving at 1:00 p.m. and returning at 2:00 p.m."

Lucille had also told Carmen that she needed speech classes because with her accent, no one could understand what she was saying. I reported Carmen's complaints to Cathy for an investigation.

Cathy notified me that in her investigation she found no fault with the manager. She said she had also taken the complaint "all the way up to legal," and they also found no fault with the manager instructing an employee to falsify her timesheet. Furthermore, the insulting statements about the employee's accent were viewed as a coaching opportunity. *I know, I know, the White woman from the South of a particular age didn't mean any harm.*

The Third and Most Horrific Case

This case for me was by far the most horrific. We hired a Black Teller Supervisor who had previously worked at Walgreens. A White male Banker asked him if he was enjoying his new job and happy not to still be selling drugs. The employee complained to me and Human Resources that he felt targeted and labeled a drug dealer because he was a Black man.

After the investigation, Cathy called me. I was in my car and immediately turned on my recorder—*so I thought*. I never pressed the red record button to start the recorder. *Not pressing that red button turned out to be a costly error and a turning point for me in everything going forward.* Cathy said she talked to the Banker, and she agreed with him that he "meant no harm." *Here we go again: they meant no harm.* Her reason was that the Banker only asked the question because the Black man had worked at Walgreens, and Walgreens has a pharmacy.

She went on to say that she understood and thought this was a reasonable question and assumption because when someone tells her they work at Walgreens, she also assumes they work in the pharmacy.

Then she asked me, "Don't you agree?"

I said "NO!!! I never think of pharmacy when someone says they work at Walgreens. Are you telling me you think a pharmacologist left his job at Walgreens to be a Teller Supervisor at a bank?"

Cathy then tried to rationalize with me and defend the White employee by saying when she thinks of Walgreens, she thinks of a drugstore. Again, I said NO!!! That is not what I think of when someone says they work at Walgreens. She finally said, "You need to tell him there is no finding of discrimination, and he needs to just get over it."

I thought that I was going to blow a gasket. I said, "**I WILL NOT tell him to just 'get over it,'** and we CAN NOT decide whether or not the Black employee was offended or felt discriminated against." I was clearly upset. Cathy then said she would call him herself and give him the results of the investigation.

Cathy Danish later denied ever saying that "he should just get over it," and it was no surprise they took her word over mine.

19
Reflections of Wisdom

Having been raised in a hostile environment, I knew and recognized hostile environments, and I knew there would be retaliation when reporting incidents of unfairness or creating boundaries. Either way, racism— *The Black Cost*—was alive, well, accepted, excused, and defended in this bank.

After all, they did say they were taking a risk by hiring people who didn't look like them.

My experiences with Human Resource Departments here and in other banks made me cautious. I've recognized that the HR representatives of banks are not there for your benefit, so I learned never to confide in them. They appear to be in place *only* to protect the senior management team. They keep records of every conversation you have with them and manipulate and use those conversations against you at their will.

You can be distracted by the Danas of the world, the Mean Girls of the South, and the people like Cathy Danish who have their own personal issues to deal with when they try to inflict harm on you. *Or* you can keep your focus on what is most beneficial for you and not be distracted by the noise of other people's drums.

PART IV: PAID IN FULL

20
A Done Deal

I t was March, and by now Dana's attacks over the past five months had become second nature to me.

Shortly after that trip to see Mommy and the rental car call, I injured my knee. While I had to adjust to the pain in my body, I did not get as much grace to slow the demands of my life.

I was making my morning shake, and when I turned around to grab a glass, I heard a loud pop in my knee. Falling to the floor, with tears running down my face, I crawled across the kitchen floor to pull myself up on a chair. After several minutes, mentally checking to see if I could stand, I got up and limped around to continue to get ready for work. Fortunately, this was an office day, and my drive to my office from the apartment was only six minutes.

Once in the office, I called my doctor and explained the pain I was experiencing, and he requested that I immediately come in for an X-ray—which was the next day. I continued to work from my office the entire day, hobbling around as necessary. I notified Dana of the incident and went for my X-ray. I called Dana after the X-ray and explained that the results would be back in two days. Dana said I needed to submit a short-term disability claim. Without having the results, this was premature for me. I told her I would use my vacation days until I got the results back.

When I received my X-ray results, I was told that I had torn my ACL. I notified Human Resources to apply for short-term disability. The representative told me I'd already filed a short-term disability claim. I said no, I have not. The representative said she would look into it and get back to me.

She called me back to say that Sara had initiated my short-term disability without my knowledge, consent, or notification. It was initiated two days earlier on the day I told Dana I would use vacation days until I got the X-ray results. Dana knew that short-term disability would automatically eliminate all vacation time.

The final nails were being hammered into my coffin. They were coming after me with a vengeance. I was floored, angry, and upset, but not confused. I was quite aware this was their final play in destroying my career. Dana had been at my throat for months, and she finally had the ammunition she needed to cut me off from what was rightfully mine. She had all the power on her side, but I still had some fight left in me. I was so upset that I contacted the Employee Support Team and explained to them what had happened to me and what was still happening to me: the discrimination I was experiencing at work including this forced short-term disability claim by Sara—I'm sure at the direction of Dana. Employee Support was no support at all. Employee Relations referred me to a therapist. I saw her weekly for the next six months.

In counseling, my therapist tried to unpack and understand why I was under this attack from Dana. She initially prescribed temporary time off, both for my physical and emotional healing, but as we continued to uncover the issues, she finally said my workplace environment, if not changed, would continue to cause me emotional harm. Finally, she diagnosed that I was in a toxic, racist, and discriminatory environment and said that if I continued to stay there, I was at risk of losing more than my career. I had not considered what else had been lost other than the opportunities I was never able to get. I had also not considered what more I had to lose at this point other than my retirement. Resilience was a part of my makeup. I lived to accommodate, work around obstacles, and find solutions. I struggled to accept that there would be no way around this—or around Dana.

In the interim, my medical doctor said that this was not a simple injury, and I was placed in a full-leg cast. The injury was to my right leg, my driving leg. I eventually had to apply for long-term disability. Even after sending pictures of my leg in the full cast and submitting all required doctors' and physical therapy reports, they denied my claim. I spoke with Employee Relations, and the representative said they always deny the first claim so just resubmit it. I did. It was denied the second time. I then went through several hearings and reviews, medical requests, and documents. It was denied again and again. Now unable to drive, with no income, and because I was on short-term disability, I also lost my month of vacation time.

Just like that, my forty-three-year banking career was free falling, and I had no way of stopping it.

I finally sought out an attorney to see what my legal rights were in this case. Her recommendation was to seek a settlement, and we sent the bank a pre-litigation settlement proposal.

As I look back I still can't believe how brainwashed I'd been. Even my pre-litigation settlement proposal was in favor of the bank. I asked for the usual mutual clauses; a general release; a neutral reference to future employers; attorney fees; a three-year back pay differential I lost as a result of the withheld resources; liquidated damages; and two years (to my early retirement age) front pay.

Despite all I had suffered, I never even asked for my medical coverage, which they continually denied. I still respected authority. I still wanted to "be a big girl" and not cause any problems. I still wanted to be accepted. Still wanted to accommodate. And I was still overlooked.

It was all denied. They rejected my proposal.

21
The Final Expense

Left with no other recourse, I filed my complaint with the state Equal Employment Opportunity Commission (EEOC).

I also included the cases of racism by Cathy, who denied ever saying the employee should "just get over" his complaint for being labeled a drug dealer because he was Black. Of all of the calls I recorded, this was the one recording on which I had not pushed the red record button. It was her word against mine. I had no way to confirm it.

"Poor and Uneducated Inhabitants"

The bank's attorney responded to EEOC that the citizens—predominantly Black—of my region were "poor and uneducated inhabitants," and that I was a big Black woman who touted my Ivy League education, and I had no basis for my claim of discrimination since the time to file a claim is three hundred days. *So? It wasn't that I was not discriminated against; I just took too long to report them.*

The irony of this racist and derogatory response is that none of my colleagues or employees ever knew my educational credentials. The only people who had access to those records were my superiors. *However, was I supposed to have some guilt about my credentials?*

They further defended my salary—or lack thereof—by referencing what they deemed as lower salaries of other employees. They then used a former Black employee as an example of a person of color who had a higher salary but again failed to disclose the details. The employee they referenced was a former Market Manager from the acquired bank, and her salary was never adjusted because she left before the one-year stipulation to find a job within her salary range. She resigned saying she "could not continue to watch Dana and Sara destroy 'good employees' careers."

Additionally, their attorney's letter accused me of cherry-picking the racial incidents I cited. I didn't understand the accusation of cherry-picking.

I cited my own racial experiences. *Whose racial incidents could I cite, but my own?*

Although they said they encouraged and supported the internal promotion and growth of their employees and confirmed that I had always met or exceeded my goals in every job I held and had always shown up in the top percentage of employees, their final disparage was to demonize me by negatively enumerating every internal position I had applied for. I hadn't realized these opportunities were only for the privileged. *But, hadn't I?*

My response to the EEOC was that every act of discrimination didn't have to be a noose left on my desk or a burning cross in my yard. Being described as a "poor and uneducated inhabitant" and a "big Black woman" is discriminatory, retaliatory, slanderous, derogatory, and inflammatory in itself.

EEOC granted me the right to move forward with litigation— something that is not easily attained. When I read the term "poor and uneducated inhabitants" in their response to the EEOC, I knew there was no shame in their discriminating and racist practices.

In response, Dana escalated the process to post my job.

22
The Retaliation

The sequence of events that happened next was appalling, and I didn't fail to push the *red button* when I made sure to record every one of these calls.

June 22 - Thursday I notified Janet in HR that my cast would be removed in three weeks, and I would have a return date. She said she would leave it as is and get back to me the following week.

July 13 – Friday I notified Janet that on Monday, July 16, my doctor would be sending me the Health Care Provider Form she requested.

July 16 – Monday I called Janet to get her fax number so I could send the Health Care Provider Form.

July 18 - Wednesday Janet called to notify me that she also needed a Health Care Provider form from my therapist regarding the anxiety and care treatment as well as confirmation that I would continue to meet with the therapist. Janet then commented that she was aware of the communications between my attorney and theirs.

July 19 - Thursday Janet notified me that she would be off for a few days and asked me to send my Health Care Provider form to her manager Lisa.

July 24 - Tuesday I notified Janet that the therapist canceled my appointment for the day and would return the following week. I offered to give her the letter stating I was under the therapist's care. She asked how long I thought I'd be unable to drive. I told her I would be getting a cortisone shot to relieve the pain the following day. I also offered to work from home.

July 25 - Wednesday at 7:00 a.m., Janet and Lisa called to inform me that my job was being posted the following day and that I had until January to apply for another position; however, if a Regional Manager position was available, I would get it. The retaliation was unabashedly blatant. There were only eight Regional Manager positions in my area of the

South. The writing was on the wall and I knew the chances of one becoming available within six months were next to impossible. *I was right.*

July 26 – Thursday Ten days after I filed my EEOC claim, my position was posted.

July 27 – Friday Dana interviewed my Sales Manager for the position—whom Dana continually described as someone "who is not now and never will be a Regional Manager."

July 30 – Monday Dana notified my Sales Manager that she had the job. Just like that, my position was filled.

As a manager, I had experienced similar replacement scenarios where we'd taken as much and oftentimes more than a year to post a person's position. I had expected that they would at least review the medical records they requested before posting my job.

A process that took me five months, several candidate rounds of panel interviews, and an interview with the Territory Manager. Now positioned to move in for the kill, while gunning to destroy me and my career, it took Dana only two days to interview, hire, and promote someone whom she identified as "not now and never will be a Regional Manager" into my job, ensuring that I had no opportunity to return. Also, since my Sales Manager was bi-racial, I believe it was also a façade for Dana to use to cover up her own discriminatory behavior.

Retaliation was immediate; my hands were tied, and my career was over as quickly as someone beheaded by the release of a guillotine.

This was just the beginning of the end.

The Last Nail

I filed for unemployment benefits. Dana denied and rejected my unemployment claim three times. I then had to go to a hearing with the State Department of Employment Services and explain why they should reverse that decision. *I won the appeal.* My reward was an unemployment benefit of $132 per week, with a maximum benefit of $4,200. I went from a six-figure salary to not even being granted the maximum unemployment benefit based on my salary. I was screwed at every turn. I didn't win. Dana won. Once again, the Mean Girls of the South, under Dana's leadership, succeeded in destroying another career. *This time mine.*

Unwilling to deplete my retirement savings on legal fees, unable to locate an attorney who would take my case pro bono, and having been stripped by the bank of all of my financial resources, I was unable to move forward with my EEOC litigation.

With no other recourse, I submitted my acknowledgment of their constructive discharge.

23
White Flag Down

Final Deposit

The ease of the bank's use of discriminatory and derogatory language and their stated beliefs about people of color being "uneducated inhabitants" certainly, in my experience, created a hostile work environment. This was the culture, and it appalls me that they use the backs of the very people that they slander and dehumanize to grow their business. *It appalls me that I stayed.*

Laughably, they accused me of having disdain for people of color, yet they accepted every White Regional Manager's refusal to live in my region with people of color yet demanded that I live there as a condition of my promotion to Regional Manager. It appears the disdain was theirs.

"See Something Say Something" was the new mantra from the top (CEO–Amy). It was rather oxymoronic because the information was always sought after, however, the whistleblower would always be punished. So, nobody ever said anything. The notification that my job would be posted came within ten days of my filing my complaint with EEOC. This type of whistleblowing (see something, say something) was a prime example of how the bank subliminally threatened and made employees afraid to bring awareness to anything.

I had hoped that the bank's Human Resources Department would take my complaints seriously, take constructive steps to address my concerns, and remedy the toxic and discriminatory environment, but they only swept the issues I raised further under the rug.

Amy, the CEO, had stated that her goal and desire was to create great employee experiences as well as to bring diversity to the leadership of the bank. In a final attempt to get the justice I deserved, employing her "See Something, Say Something" motto, I penned this email to Amy.

To: Amy, CEO of the Retail Bank

You once stated that you recognize that leadership at the top is devoid of diversity and that you have a desired goal of inclusiveness and plan to change this narrative.

My experiences as a person of color at this bank have not been great. As you review my history you can know firsthand what it's like for a person of color at this company. Given the absence of diversity at the top, I am also sure that many people of color here are having or have had similar experiences to mine.

Finally, as you consider the "reputational risk" to the bank, you must know that many careers are being destroyed at the hands of market leadership in the South. Perhaps by taking a closer look at the market, you will gain some understanding of the excessive turnover they experience.

I am saying something in the hopes that my experience inspires you to hastily implement your "desired goal of inclusiveness."

Amy responded that she received my email and would look into it. The written response from the bank's attorney was more slander.

While my EEOC complaint was overtly ignored by the bank, there was an immediate influx of "taking a risk" and hiring several people of color into leadership positions above the Branch Manager level—starting with my position—and Dana was relocated to another state.

24
Reward in a Different Currency

At this point, I was knocked down literally and physically by the bank, and my career was long over. I didn't share the issues from work with my family. *Why would I?* They never expressed any care about my well-being. My only value to them was in my ability to finance and take responsibility for their issues. I don't even think they noticed I was no longer working.

Mommy's Illness

Mommy's health was quickly declining. She just sat in her bedroom deteriorating. After many calls to the state, I was finally able to get her twelve hours of care. It was a little relief, but she was still alone for twelve hours and wasn't sleeping. I was spending as much time as I could traveling to New York to visit Maurier and to make sure Mommy had the best care given the situation.

There would be times when Mommy would call me in the early morning hours, screaming, asking me to please help her. Too embarrassed and unable to verbalize what help she needed. But I knew she'd spent the past twelve hours sitting in her urine and feces.

I spent more time than I care to count in the shower crying about her circumstances, my circumstances, and my inability to change any of it. *All of it.* I don't know; they were all so intertwined.

I begged and begged Mommy to come and live with me, giving her all the reasons it would help her. She finally agreed. I arranged to have medical transportation bring her from New York to our home. Everything was scheduled and ready to go. On the day she was to be transported, she canceled and said she changed her mind. I was so sad and distraught. I didn't know what else to do. I was heartbroken.

During her last stay at a rehabilitation facility, Mommy was diagnosed with lung cancer. The doctor said there was nothing else they could do, but he wanted our consent to perform a biopsy. I asked why he would do a biopsy if there was nothing that could be done. Please, just leave her in peace.

Once Mommy stopped eating, a hospice representative came to speak with us—me, Andre, and Deborah—the one rare time that the three of us were there together. We gathered around outside Mommy's hospital room door as the representative told us about the hospice care process. There was nothing else they could do for Mommy except to keep her comfortable so she wouldn't be in pain. The representative said she could hear us. If we had anything to say to her, now was the time to say it.

I couldn't help but remember that earlier hospital stay when the doctor told us to come right away if we wanted to see her. Deborah started crying hysterically and said, "Whatever y'all decide," and went back into Mommy's room. Andre and I went to the conference room down the hall to discuss and sign the hospice agreement. Andre said he would go along with whatever I decided, once again leaving all the decision-making up to me because, at the end of the day, I believe they didn't want to be responsible for anything to do with Mommy dying.

We each took turns going into her room to say our last goodbyes. When it was my turn, tears welled up in my eyes, and all I could say was, "Mommy, I'm so sorry I left you and lived my life without you. I'm sorry I abandoned you. I love you so much. I've always loved you."

And all she could muster with her shallow breath was, "I love you too."

I went back home planning to return in a couple of weeks. Unfortunately, Mommy passed a couple of days before my return flight was scheduled.

It seemed Mommy spent all her life trying to do things that would have pleased Nana. She seemed to be willing herself to die at the age of eighty because Nana died at eighty, as if she was seeking her approval even from the grave. She appeared to have simply given up on trying to be happy. Mommy died two weeks before her eighty-first birthday.

Andre and our niece were at the rehab center when Mommy passed. At least she wasn't alone. Andre called me. I gathered my things and got on a plane to make the arrangements. I notified Deborah and Andre of the time of the appointment at the funeral home.

Deborah said, "I'm not going to be able to come to the funeral home. I can't take it. It's too much for me. Whatever you decide because you're the oldest."

Andre said, "Okay. I'll be there."

Maurier and I got to the funeral home and waited for Andre to show up; he never came. *He's always been good for saying he was going to do something and then just ghost you. It's his way of not dealing with a situation.* With Maurier, my rock, by my side, I proceeded to make the funeral arrangements. I felt like the thirteen-year-old again who just wanted to hug Mommy and say that everything was going to be okay. The thirteen-year-old who was responsible for taking care of my mother. That was fine because it allowed me to take care of her final resting place and make sure she had the send-off she deserved. To take care of her and give her the love she didn't appear to have in life. Giving her in death the care she refused from me in life.

Two days before Mommy's funeral, Maurier and I came down with the worst case of Covid, and we couldn't go to her funeral. My body felt awful, but my soul was even heavier than anything I'd ever carried. I wanted nothing more than to savor those final moments with my mother. I wanted to lay down all those desires there with her. I needed to mourn all the things I never got to do with and for her. I wanted to sit in the space with her . . . just one last time. But I didn't get to be there.

I even asked Maurier to just drive me to the cemetery so that I could sit in the car and watch from afar, but he refused. As you've already discovered, I am not a good beggar or negotiator for my needs. Plus, I could never explain to Maurier the need I had to just be in the vicinity of my mother's body one last time. Neither he nor anyone could ever really understand the unspoken bond I had with my mother because we were so estranged.

I had no closure with my mother. I didn't get to experience those final moments or be responsible for everything going as I planned. Maybe it was as it was supposed to be—those last moments at her hospital bed with us professing our love for each other.

As she did when Daddy died, in my absence, Brandi stepped in and made sure everything at Mommy's funeral had gone exactly as I had planned. Brandi is more like her father in many ways, however, when she displays my characteristics, her strength surprises me, and I realize how much like me she really is.

It was the same with both my parents: on their hospital deathbeds, in our profession of love for each other, I said, "I love you." With Daddy, although he could not talk, he made the motions—pointing to his heart, crossing his arms around his chest, and then pointing to me. With Mommy, it was her shallow breath saying, "I love you too."

Maybe those goodbyes were enough. Maybe that was the closure. Perhaps that was a good thing—as good as it gets. Rewards in a different currency.

25
Reflections of Wisdom

Without a second thought, I relocated four times in three years. I was always so damn accommodating. Always wanting to do the right thing. Always wanting to "be a big girl" and follow the rules. I didn't understand that the expense of my accommodation would be the recognition I so rightfully deserve. I didn't know I was paying into the very systems that were oppressing me. I thought the opposite. I thought that I could give more, and it would be returned to me. Instead, the more I gave and the harder I worked, the more I was used and the less I received.

Accommodation was the only conflict resolution style that I was reared to embody. It wasn't safe, it wasn't perfect, but it was certainly normal.

Oddly enough, my need to accommodate was first to be invisible, but then to be visible.

This "Big Girl" from the projects in Harlem didn't have any carrots to begin life with. I was the donkey that had the carrot dangled before me, only to overlook the muddy puddles I had to walk in, the extra hoops I had to jump through, and the endless miles I walked without complaint, *at least not out loud.* I ignored the pain in my body and the pain in my soul because I was chasing the prize I thought was before me. I recognized that the load I carried only got harder. But the golden prize was right there. *If I worked a little harder I could have it.* I didn't have anything to lose but everything to gain. That damn carrot looked so good. I *knew* if I kept going, I could get it. *I had to get it.*

In my forced retirement, I've learned that blessings are not always what God has given you, but often times it is what He's taken away. Having my career snatched away suddenly and unexpectedly forced me to take a step back and take a hard look at my life. I started counting my blessings. I have not missed any meals. I have not missed any mortgage payments. I don't have any debt, I still travel the world. No weapon formed against me has prospered. What Dana did to harm me didn't touch me. Instead, God used her hatred to elevate me.

So, maybe like Moses, the mission was never for me to see the Promised Land, but the mission was instead for me to make a path available for all of those who followed me.

About the Author

It is a true balancing act to protect yourself and realize your dreams because there is always someone willing to destroy you. I've experienced the struggles of living in a single-parent household. I'm not in hiding. I don't pretend I have something or to be something that I am not. I'm very proud to say that I come from Harlem. People make their own judgments anyway.

I enjoy using my talent, skills, and education to help others. I give financial seminars at churches and other institutions and resources to my friends when they request it. People often ask, "Do you know how much money you can make? Why don't you charge?" My answer is simply it's not about money for me. It's about how good I feel when I can pay it forward and bless someone else. You never know when a little help or act of kindness will help someone flourish in their own way.

My earlier passion for traveling and real estate led me to obtain my real estate license and open a travel and event planning business. I welcome your visit to portcityeventsplanner.com.

In my leisure, you will find me basking in the sun of one of my four favorite pastimes: taking long drives with my husband, having weekly lunches with my daughter, reading in my sunroom overlooking the lake, or having pizza parties with my grandchildren as they run back and forth, laughing and playing in the pool, demanding that I take videos of them.

I finally got my dream house overlooking the water. My plan and dream house was an apartment in a high-rise building overlooking the Hudson River. God's plan for me was a custom-built home overlooking a lake with a swimming pool and a dock on the canal. God has literally moved me from the projects to the lake house.

When I look back over my life, I would like to believe that the suffering and sacrifices I've endured as a Black woman in the banking industry and in my world were well worth the pain if they've allowed me to add value and help someone else be better than I was. Do better than I did. I pray that this book does that for someone else—for so many others.

My life is good. God is good.

Author's Credentials

Education
Master of Science in Industrial and Labor Relations, Cornell University
Bachelor of Science in Business Administration, York College (CUNY)
Minor in Accounting and Psychology
Licenses and Certificates Held
NASD Series 6, 63 & 7 (National Association of Securities Dealers)
New Jersey & Pennsylvania Life & Variables Insurance Licenses
Certified Adult Trainer and Developer
New York & North Carolina Realtor
Member of the National Association of Realtors and Real Estate Brokers
IATAN Accredited Travel Advisor
Certified Wedding and Events Planner
NY, NJ, and NC Notary
Affiliations
Cornell University Alumni
York College Alumni, Inc.
Harlem Hospital Community Advisory Board
Jackie Robinson Park Conservancy, Inc
Member of Leadership Strategies
Member of Toastmasters
Accomplishments
York College Alumni, Inc (Association)
President of the Association
Chairperson of Fundraising and Planning Committee
Director of Project Literacy Program
Executive Director to Public Affairs and Nominating Committees
Community
Harlem Hospital Community Advisory Board
Chairperson, of the Board of Directors & Public Hearing Committee (partnered with elected officials to keep the hospital open)
Chaired the By-Laws Committee and re-wrote the first set of By-Laws in 30 years
Jackie Robinson Park Conservancy, Inc
    Secretary of the Board of Directors

    Chairperson of Events Planning, Business Development, and Fundraising
Family Promise of Monroe County, PA (transition families from homelessness to mainstream)
Board Member, Vice President, President
Pocono Services for Families and Children—Board Member
United Way of Monroe County, PA—Funds Distribution Committee Member
PA and NC Homeowners Association Board member and Treasurer

Acknowledgments
All of you inspired me to share my legacy

Brandi, my daughter, you've changed my life in every way and your bias always makes me feel like the best mother in the whole world. Beautiful girl, don't forget that you are a princess. Don't ever sell yourself cheap. You were made for great things.

My grandbabies, Alaysia, Wesly, Jonah, Alani, Aubrey, and Emmanuel, you love me so unconditionally and inspire me to smile and see the world through brand-new eyes. King, Empress, Zion, I look forward to one day developing a relationship with you.

Jonathan, my son-in-law, I put you through a great trial. You are a good father and have a good heart at your core. It's that which makes me love you as a son.

Maurier, my son, I see you because I've been you. You have the biggest and kindest heart. Set boundaries, protect your heart, and love yourself more than you love anyone else. Seek your own happiness above all others and above all else.

Tyson, my son, the world is your oyster. Put in the work, get the pearl, continue to transform, and be the great person I know you will be.

Alex, Denise, and Greg, my siblings, I don't get to say it to you face to face enough. I love you unconditionally.

My nieces and goddaughters, Amaya, Atina, Desiree, Jadia, Joi, Khadejah, Natanee, Roxanne, Sharmaca, Simone, S i m o n e , and Whitney, as you've quietly observed me from afar, I pray that my life serves you in some small way on your journey to be greater women than I ever aspired to be.

Carol, in forty-eight years we've slayed a lot of dragons together. I will leave it at that.

Oscar, it's been fifty-three years, and you've been like a big brother to me—always there and never judging. I am grateful to have you in my life.

Melvina, in the three short years I've known you, you've taught me that dammit if I want to change my mind and do something different every day, it is my God-given right to do so, and I should not leave this life regretting not doing something simply because I didn't try it.

Maurier, My Hero, my sunshine, my rock. I believe that relationships are like a year of seasons. They have ebbs and flows. The summer is hot and steamy and you can't seem to get enough of each other, and then the fall sets in and you literally fall into a routine; and then comes winter and no matter where you set the thermostat, one of you is cold while the other one is hot, and just when you're at your wit's end, here comes spring and everything blossoms, and you're just happy to be with the one person who knew you through the seasons. I am happy you are the person I'm sharing this year of seasons with.

To my family, my friends, and my foes, thank you for the color you've added to this leg of my journey